# Dancing
## on the *Waters*
### Stepping Out of the Boat

Dave McDaniel

Published by Aglow International
PO Box 1749
Edmonds, WA 98020-1749
www.aglow.org

Printed in the United States of America

Library of Congress Cataloging-in-Publication Data

Cover design by Aglow International

# Table of Contents

# Acknowledgments

I want to thank Jane Hansen Hoyt, president and CEO of Aglow International, for her leadership and influence in my life. Without your influence, Jane, I would not have been captured by God's intentions for men and women working together as one reconciled by God. You also introduced me to a deeper passionate walk with God, and I am grateful to serve beside you.

I could never have experienced an understanding of how to grow in my identity had it not been for Graham Cooke. You are a voice for the times, and your teaching and declarations have influenced the body of this writing.

A special thanks to Kay Rogers, who has guided me through the many logistical turns of this project. You have also modeled for me what a true servant leader is, and I consider you my colleague and friend.

My editor, Jane Campbell, has taught me the intricacies of writing, organization, and voice in these entries. You have been patient, kind, and very encouraging.

My friend Rick Allen and the Creative Services Department at Aglow International have been instrumental in the design and artwork of the book, and your talent is appreciated.

I especially honor Nancy, my partner in marriage and ministry. You have protected my heart from the very first day we met, and you have taught me how to dream and appropriate truth in every facet of my life. You are my greatest encourager, and I love you more today than ever.

# Acknowledgements

# *Introduction*

As I have concluded that there has to be more than what I am experiencing in my relationship with You, Lord, I have been on a journey of amazing and unbelievable growth. You have brought me from the desert to the boat to the sea. All along this journey of the past 36 months, I have experienced Your marvelous goodness and faithfulness toward me. You didn't see a man who was broken, sidetracked, or shipwrecked. You saw what I was to become. Graciously, You brought me on this journey of dreams and unreachable destinations through relationship. The closer I pressed in to find out who You really are, the more You revealed who I was to become. You met me in the place where I was, and I didn't have to climb a mountain of holiness to get an audience with You.

For sure, You came to me because of my heart's cry. I wanted more of You as I explored who You created me to be. I found that the more I pressed into Your heart, the more I fell in love with You. Consequently, I discovered who You said I was created to be. As I started my quest, I moved from glory to glory, because my expectations of You grew at every level. I am not a man of great words, but I am a man with a great heart toward You. All I knew was to write and journal to You. Our conversation resulted in desperate times of my unquenchable desire for You. Your words to me are the foundation of who I am. The distant accusations of who I used to be were overtaken by the glorious sound of heaven declaring my persona—my true identity as You see me.

I penned these words at the beginning of our journey. Do You remember them, Lord?

## *I Want To*

Your holy presence dwells in me, and I will not be shaken or convinced otherwise. I desire to be Your temple that can house the fullness of Your presence. Full of wisdom and power, I want to be that vessel You depend on to release Your kindness, goodness, and love. Wash over me and cleanse me of all unbelief, doubt, and complacency. For such a time as this, I have been created.

Your using me to house Your glory requires far-reaching understanding, and the fullness and richness of Your knowledge are much more than I can house—but I want to.

Your vastness and greatness are more than I can understand—but I want to.

Your purpose in the earth through me is more than I can wrap my head around—but I want to.

As I begin this uncharted journey, increase in me Your desires, that they may become my only focus. I await the refreshing waterfalls of Your mighty, powerful presence to cleanse and preserve me, washing away all blindness, sickness, insecurity, and complacency. Refresh me with a greater hunger and thirst after Your heart, and cause me to know who I really am and the purpose for which I was created.

## *To the Reader*

If you are looking for a short story of conversations with God about the journey that will fulfill your ultimate purpose—the one you were created for—this will be one model that works.

If you are searching for a deeper understanding of who you are and how God sees you, this book will be life-giving to you.

If you are tired of being immobilized, stuck in the boat of life, and you want to step out of the boat and explore the limitlessness of God's intentions for you, I invite you to grow into the place of dancing on the waters with Jesus as He celebrates your identity with you. Read this book by personalizing these conversations and dance with the Star.

Every day is brand-new and every situation has the miraculous nugget of your identity attached to it. You cannot fail, and you cannot disappoint God in this process of relationship. He has a remarkable destiny for you that is far beyond the realm of your own thinking; you are way too important to pass by.

As you read this book, I declare over you that your life will not merely change but be transformed into a brand-new image. As you bring your honest heart to God, I proclaim that you will enjoy the liberty and confidence to discuss every situation openly with Him. God wants to have a conversation with you that will change your perspective, empowering you to change and become victorious over every obstacle and challenge. I speak over your life that you will see shifts and new beginnings that will supersede ones from the days before. All God wants from you is a searching heart that will dare to get out of the boat of past understanding and accept His invitation to take His hand and dance with Him on the waters.

Have you grown complacent in your level of relationship with God, but you have a heart for something much greater? Do you want more but cannot put your finger on what it is? Do you feel a sense of urgency that has caused you to search for the next level of God's best? He is up to something big, and you are part of His plan. I invite you to crawl onto Papa's lap, place your head on His heart, and listen to the rhythm of His intentions for you.

A sound from heaven has announced your name. Come, and let God breathe on you.

## *For Reflection*

What do you want out of this journey? Write it down, and in the near future you will see how far God has brought you in your understanding of your true identity and His remarkable love for you.

# 1

# Burying the Old Nature

## It Is Finished

You crucified my old nature when You hung on the cross. You did not just die for me; You died as me. Every area of my old life is dead. I am dead to sin. You are no longer dealing with my sin; You already dealt with it on the cross. Now You are dealing with my righteousness. Not intent on just stopping me from sinning, You are committed to teaching me how to be righteous and holy.

You have brought newness of life. I have been resurrected to new life with Jesus. I am a new creation. My flesh and my old man are past tense; death has become the starting point of life. My old life, habits, and sin nature have already met their demise. You said, "It is finished." I am free from sin's dominion over me then, liberated to become like You in the power of Your resurrection. Done deal. My old sinful nature is dead and I am not giving it CPR anymore. Instead I am operating in the breath of Your glory, and my righteousness has sprung up, choking out the weeds of my old nature.

## For Reflection

1. Make a list of the characteristics from your old nature that you are still struggling with: jealousy, fear, hatred, lust, pride, and more.
2. What do these words of Jesus mean to that list: "It is finished!"
3. List the areas of your new nature in Christ. How can you walk in new life in each area?

# 2

# Crossing Over the Threshold of Destiny

## Open Doors

You have awesomely opened doors of new beginnings; they are full of fresh revelation and favor. I have crossed the threshold, stepping into the new and leaving the old behind in a journey of intimacy. You alone have opened every door, and I thank You for the immensity of my journey ahead. Take my heart and mold me like moist clay, an impressionable work. I do not know the places where I am going or how to walk the way before me. But You have brought me into this new land.

Even as I step into new places of wonder, sounds from the old, broken places try to invade. Protect my body, mind, and emotions from the devastation of the screaming accusations all around me. Spirit of God, arise in me today and deliver me from the fear of the unknown. I can do all things through Christ because it is He who strengthens me.

Show me the eternal purpose and mission of this era of exploration and discovery. Your Word is high above all things, and Your promise of protection and provision is without wavering. It is a strong tower of promise without compromise. Transform my mind with Your wondrous thoughts of life and favor, which usher in change while transforming how I see things and who I am becoming.

## Walk with Me

*To know Me is to open the door to knowledge of Me. Walking farther and farther with Me will release more and more knowledge of Me. I* AM *releasing My glory and favor over you, for the time to favor you has come. The response of the opposition is duly noted, but the door I open is final. As you have crossed this threshold, My glory will enlighten your path and blind the enemy. He loves to take shots in the dark to instill fear and chaos, hoping something will deter you. Do not be caught up in his entrapment. You have a new future ahead, taking you into your purpose for this hour. Walk with Me and be captured in My majesty. My faithfulness is a circle of protection around you. Move freely within this circle, and don't listen to the voices of the past, for they want to distract you from the moving wheel of My glory. Stay within its radius and move with My rhythm. Listen to Me this morning.*

## For Reflection

1. What does your "new land" look like in this new journey? What areas of promise is God taking you to?
2. Are there open doors to your future that your are hesitant to walk through? Why or why not?
3. Do a prophetic act of burying a symbol of your past.
4. What do you see as the difference between hearing God and listening to Him?

# 3

# I AM in Control of Your Destiny

## I AM

*Be at peace. Be at rest. Be all I have created you to be by understanding that* I AM *your source. You have said it over and over. But know it! Establish your identity by it! Release every insecurity because of it! I* AM ... *enough said. Be at peace and rest in your day today. Bring My presence to every molecule and atom. Your atmosphere is drenched in My presence because the great* I AM *is intervening on your behalf. Replace striving with rest in the confidence that it is I who go before you. It is I who come behind you with all My goodness and mercy. And it is I who hold you by your right hand and defend My purpose in you. I* AM *your advocate and strong tower of refuge. Rest in Me as you leave the rest to Me. It is I. Do not be afraid. Do not fear.* I AM *is here.*

*Here* I AM, *child.* I AM *overwhelmed by the sweet-smelling aroma of your love song to Me. I cannot help but bless you and keep you, protect you and guide you, because I have sung My song of jealousy over you. It is My jealousy that causes Me to respond the way I do. As you turn all your affections toward Me, they meet with My combustible jealousy and together create waves of glory.*

*You are coming into a new place of authority and love. With authority come power and blessing. I have a new beginning chapter of your life waiting. This one is designed to propel you into your purpose. Do not box Me in to expectations of meager possibilities. Open up and release your faith to receive abundance.* I AM *sending it from sources you would never have thought possible. Come to My table. I have several gifts packaged just for you. They will custom-fit your next purpose.*

*To experience what I have for you, you cannot make it happen. But you can delay it if you choose not to focus and listen.* I AM *infusing you with confidence for this next journey.* I AM *Christ in you, the hope and expectation of glory.*

I AM *placing in you a hunger and thirst for Me as never before. You* read the Scripture that "if riches increase"—and they will, compatible with My purpose—"do not set your heart upon them" (Psalm 62:10, NASB). Resources have been assigned for purpose, not pleasure. Keep your eyes focused keenly on your affection toward Me, and you will not be entangled by the temptation to chase after anything else. Attune your ear to listen, and you will hear the reasons and know the targets of the prosperity I AM bringing you.

No one is safe from My abundance. I AM placing what is left of your impoverished lifestyle in the crucible. I will raise you up to believe exactly what I say. Boundless, limitless faith and resources will combine to fund the end-time harvest. I have already chosen you from long, long ago, earmarked for this time in history. Stand up straight, hold your head up, walk with confidence. You are My kid!

I AM healing you now. I AM moving you into the realm of the supernatural where you will speak and it shall be done by your Father in heaven. You will speak the thought conceived by the Holy Spirit from the nighttime, and it shall be activated through you the next morning. I need you in this time and season to activate release. Do not worry about the petty criticism or judgment around you. It is a benefit of the extra blessing I am bestowing on you. Let it refine you and shape your confidence in Me in such a way that the stormy conditions around you are calmed into perfect peace in the sea of rest.

Find delight in everything around you, for it all serves My purpose for you. Holy Spirit is with you to speak confidence. Listen to Him and be purposeful in your responses. I will not let you fail. We have no time left for that. By the holy, eternal purposes of My heart, I crown you with the authority and heritage to walk as My son, privileged to receive all that I have to offer. You have graduated and completed the requirements assigned to this new beginning. Be blessed, and be a blessing. We will do this together.

## For Reflection

1. In what areas of your life have you been striving?
2. What would you like God to be for you in these areas? How can you partner with Him?
3. What is the passion of your heart for your future? How does it line up with your prophetic words and with what the Word of God says?

# 4

# *New Clothes of Grace*

## Help Me Become New

Father, I come to You with the remnants of my old garments. I have allowed myself to wear them in times of weakness. Momentary lapses attack my confidence to operate in the new man. Forgive me and reestablish my coming and going. Direct me toward what is missing in my relationship with You and empower me to behave accordingly. I hate self-condemnation and guilt. The shame they bring obliterates confidence and progress. Feeding the flesh sucks the Spirit dry in me, and the old man nature cannot profit me in this new place.

Wind of God, You are blowing through the earth today with greater speed and intensity. Blow over me, Holy Spirit, and be released through me. Gust away the guilt and condemnation of mistakes and shortcomings. As Your wind blows, lift me higher to where the atmosphere of heaven suffocates my faulty thinking. Instead of living in self-condemnation, guilt, and the shame of poor decisions, You are calling me up into my Christ-filled persona. You are not calling me out in my behavior; You are calling me up into my identity. You don't see the shortcomings of the present; You see what I am becoming.

## Outrageous Grace

*Outrageous grace is yours. I have never left you nor rescinded what I have said. My word establishes purpose. Come up higher to see My perspective of your identity. You see every mistake as a big stumblingblock, but I don't focus on your mistakes. That is because I have been upgrading your righteousness in Christ. View every mistake as a golden opportunity to focus on how I see you—the finished product—and come into agreement with that.*

*Do not establish your identity by fixating on the performance of your walk in holiness. Just be holy as I AM holy. Just be, through My gift* and My permission. No amount of striving to be holy can work. Your holiness comes from Me, not from the rituals of performance. Receive My holiness. I have set you apart from your performance and crowned you with My righteousness, which permits you to be holy. I have placed you in Christ and Christ in you. My work is already complete in you. You are just walking out the process.

Do you see My grace a little more clearly now? You have already been separated from sin. My grace is the source of power to replace old man behavior with new habits of righteousness. I AM taking the very thing that the enemy has used as a strategy in the past to defeat you, and redirecting it as an instrument of grace to move you closer to your persona. Every negative is really a positive because of the rich process of transformation. I do not condone sin or approve of the devastating consequences of its hold over you. But it has a hold upon you only when you allow it to live in you.

Each day when you come to Me, you will notice that My grace has already cleaned up the messes left behind. In their place, I have released upgrades in your life to overcome those areas in the future. See every upgrade as your weapon to eventually replace your old sin habits and enable you to abide in this high place of process and understanding.

All is well, child. I killed off the power of sin once and for all. Love the learning, and be transformed into your identity through the constant renewal of your mind. Behold, all things have become new. Change your language to reflect the new man inside you. Listen to what he says about you, and begin to talk that language as a lifestyle.

I AM a habitational God. When you view Me as One who visits only when you are "good," your perception becomes faulty through old man thinking, as if something you do could ever cause Me to leave you. When you finally understand that I AM with you 24-7, you will understand that sin habits cannot separate Me from you. They can, however, separate you from truly understanding how I see you. It is time, child, to make a decision to come up higher in your thinking, and to know that I will never lift My hand of favor and grace from you. I AM committed to the end, and so are you.

## For Reflection

1. Can you feed the flesh of your old man and feed your spirit at the same time? Explain.
2. Does putting on the new man mean you never make mistakes? Instead of living in self-condemnation, how does God see your mistakes?
3. How would you define God's grace?

# 5

## Victory Has Been Assigned

### Teach Me to Receive Your Fire

I give You my undivided attention so that I can discern the seed of Your resource and favor toward me when it comes in, for You have determined it to be the key to my multiplication. I have never experienced what I am about to see. I lift up my seed today. Plant me, Father; water me and make me grow. Thank You for healing me and setting me free from all the distractions around me. I am free. We dance together now in the rhythm and beat of Your throne.

I will bring every thought into captivity to the obedience of Jesus Christ. I take the thought captive that says humanity has dominion over my destiny. I take captive all my insecurities that are based on performance in an attempt to win man's favor. I command every thought of inferiority to bow the knee to Your grace. I command every proud and haughty place of superiority to lay itself on the cross and be crucified. I operate in humility and servanthood. I trust Your loving care and promises to guard my future. Protect me from myself and from others. Establish me in Your purpose. Everything else is rubbish.

I am excellent because You are excellent. Teach me how to receive Your fire that blazes the trail before me. Open the heavens and fall onto my areas of influence with the fire of efficiency and follow-through. Reignite the fire within me to pursue everything with passion. I need to hear Your voice. I long to hear Your affirmation. I am frustrated and tired as my confidence wavers from running this race.

When You prepared Joseph, You brought him forth from the hidden place of captivity with the wisdom and anointing to lead. I anoint myself with oil to go forward in excellence and confidence. Bring those into my life who will not judge me but invest in me.

Excellence—that is what I bring. Crown me with excellence as You crown me with the beautiful mind of Christ. I am Your child of promise. Wash over me and wash my mind. Renew my mind with Yours. I need the grace that comes from Your throne. Drown out the accusations and taunts.

I have been appointed as a director of heaven on this earth. I bring heaven with me to plant and to release. Your promises are true and Your purposes unchangeable. Bring Your intentions to fruition. Show me what to do. Direct me in how to connect with my surroundings. Give me Yourself. Open up the true me.

## Holy Spirit Is Assigned to Bring You Victory

*One drop of My grace is greater than the sum of all your fears. I AM not here to condemn you or bring judgment or criticism your way. I AM. Therefore, you are. You have My DNA. Pursue the promptings of the Holy Spirit today. I have assigned Him to bring you out into victory. He is undefeated and so are you. Be confident in Him. He is Your Helper. Talk to Him throughout your day. When you have that understanding of His presence and commitment to work in your life, you will weather any storm.*

*Be confident in Him. He is busy at work transforming you into the accelerated, finished product of purpose. But you free fear to wreak havoc on you when you forget that it is not by might, nor by power, but by My Spirit. Let Me exhibit My power and extend the curtains of your dwelling by introducing others to My presence. Bring Me into view, refocus on Me, and you will be victorious over all. I AM bringing you through all this. Enjoy the learning. Don't despise and rebel because of the discomfort of the stretching. When I stretch you, I can pour more into you. Be at peace today, and remember that I AM.*

## For Reflection

1. Are you experiencing anticipation of what God has in store for you? What might those things be?
2. Has God had you in a hidden place in this past season? Ask God to show you what He has been developing in you in this time of preparation.
3. Have you allowed God to empty you in this place so He can refill you with new anointing for the new task ahead? Do so now.

# 6

## Knowing Who You Are

### Power of Identity

My identity grows stronger by overcoming. My identity upgrades who I am in the Spirit. Because I cannot become a new person by changing my behavior, I must discover the person I already am in You and behave accordingly. I fight all negativity by stepping into my identity and practicing what You see about me.

The words of Your heart are my persona, my true identity. Align my own perception of myself with Your perception of me. Show me how You see me, Father. If I don't see it, I can't become it. Once I see it, however, I will come into agreement with You and step into my identity.

I reframe my thinking to align with the mind of Christ, refusing to think from the identity of my past experiences. My warfare against the enemy is a life of fruitfulness. Every challenge the enemy brings against me, I will defeat by moving in the opposite spirit. Every situation is designed to make me more like You. When I have a promise from You, I do not wait for it to come to me. I automatically have what You have promised, and I grow into its fulfillment. My thinking is no longer challenged by the enemy, by wicked people, or by difficult circumstances. I can only be challenged by Your goodness.

### For Reflection

1. How do you think the Father sees you?
2. What do you think it means to put on the mind of Christ? Thinking from this perspective, how do you see yourself?
3. What does God's goodness look like in a difficult situation you may be facing.

# 7

# The Art of Transformation

## Chosen for Blessing

Father, You chose me before I chose You. As I ponder my purpose, I want to be woven into the fabric of Your heart, and let Your heart be woven into my purpose as I plow ahead. No more treading for survival.

Treading and plowing, I know, are two different things. Treading is remaining in my present state, satisfied with having my needs met, surviving by keeping my head above water. But plowing is working toward my purpose and inheritance, energized by the promise of that inheritance.

Teach me, Lord, how to plow and to be efficient in the place You have for me. I see new learning curves here. You know the way that I take. I am a Psalm 1 blessed man planted by the rivers of water, bringing forth fruit. In whatever I do, I prosper.

Upgrade me into a man of God for this hour. I want to catch the wave of Your purpose, the place where the power of Your presence to transform people, cities, states, nations, and atmospheres is part of my spiritual portfolio. I want to see sinners saved, the sick healed, lepers cleansed, and the dead raised. I want to operate in that glory.

This upgrade is my inheritance, and I step into places to receive its fullness. No more teasers or previews of the promise. Take me deep into the place of Your heart where my inheritance and identity blend with the intentions that only You have for me—Your intentionality.

## Transformed into My Image

*How beautiful are My dwelling places where you are changed and transformed into My image. Dwelling in Me is a lifestyle change, not an appointment to keep. Firsthand knowledge of what I AM doing is a privilege of your dwelling in Me.*

*I AM removing your limitations that hinder your ability to see, hear, and feel My intentionality. I fill every promise with My intentions, and I bend everything to bow to My will and purpose.*

*I have been changing you into your heaven-to-earth persona throughout your life. Upgrades and transformed thinking are part of this process. Through your life you have focused on the struggles associated with change. Now I AM teaching you to see as I see. When I look at you, I don't see failures or struggles. I see My victorious warrior—complete, perfect, and ready for deployment. Go forth, mighty man of valor. I have given you the upgrades to be and to become. I have activated the gifts and talents to make you the vessel of honor and trust I have designed you to be; to become perfected in fullness in Me.*

## For Reflection

1. Are you presently plowing or treading? Which of the two is life-giving, and which is life-draining? Why do you think that is?
2. What spiritual legacy would you like to leave behind when you are gone? What areas of your life require upgrades in order for you to achieve your legacy?
3. Your persona is how you are known in heaven and how God sees you as a completed work. Ask God what your persona is. Ask Him how He sees you.

# 8

# I Am Your Confidence

## Breathe on Me

Breathe upon me today. Never let me go, and never let me become separated from You. Remove my walls of insecurity and inferiority that erect seemingly impenetrable barriers to keep me from experiencing Your presence. You are my confidence, and Your most intimate thoughts are toward me continuously. I never want to be separated from my awareness of Your presence. You are committed to my development. Father, I live to be in Your presence. Squeeze my hand more tightly as I gaze into Your eyes of affirmation.

I cannot rid myself of negative thoughts by focusing on them. Instead, I make war upon them because they are dead weight. I bring You my perceptions, language, and thinking. Cause each of these to soar with certainty in who I am becoming. I can be confident because You are my confidence. I can be victorious in all things because You are my Victor. I can be the miracle in every situation because You are the Miracle-Worker working through me.

Bring my every negative thought and perception of myself into the shredder of Your Spirit. I must get out of my soul to operate in Your Spirit. It is not by might, nor by power, but by the Spirit of the Lord. Bring the shift, Lord. You have the floor. You are the sound I listen to. I am dead to negativity because I am alive in You. Christ in me is the hope of glory. My renewed mind rehearses Your perceptions and identification of me. I walk in Your fullness, not in yesterday's limitations. I am a new creation. I have a new outlook, a new inward opinion of who I am in You.

I raise my open hands in surrender. Reach out and grab my hands and bring me closer to Your side. Cause me to feel the unhindered and unobstructed closeness of Your Person. Release Your presence through Your touch. Enlarge my perceptions, increase my influence, and impart Your anointing and power to release what You have given me. Shower Your gifts over me as I lift up my gift to You. I love You.

## I Hold Your Hand

*Your true identity was first activated in your past. It was birthed and nurtured there, only to create a bridge into new discoveries of who you are becoming. When you look back at those times of the past, you will see My fingerprints on everything. But realize, child, that My hand is no longer there. My hand is in yours, leading you into this current place of destiny. Do not be afraid, anxious, self-critical, or stressed. You are with Me, remember? Do not let go of My hand.*

*I AM bringing you into your future by teaching you how to navigate every circumstance victoriously through your total dependence on Me. When stormy situations arise, and when you feel perplexed because new challenges lack needed answers, I AM the answer. These challenges are there only to establish your identity, authority, and territory. Do not be afraid or anxious; relax and rest in unwavering confidence that I AM is with you. It is My responsibility, not yours, to establish your purposes in the earth. I AM. You be. I love you, child.*

## For Reflection

1. How will you get rid of negative thoughts or negative thinking? Give some practical examples of how you can do this.
2. Picture your hand in His. You have His attention. What would you say to Him about your struggles with negativity? Tell Him.

# 9

## Called and Commissioned

### A "Suddenly" for You

*Do not become discouraged or weary in this waiting time of development. It is necessary for you to carry the weight of My glory. You have done well in shepherd fields, protecting those whom I have placed in your care. You have done well in your relationship with Me. But hear My voice that calls you out of the fields and establishes you in this fresh beginning. You are not meant to remain in the fields. It is there that you have developed ears to hear what I AM saying and eyes to see in the Spirit. In this time of intense training, you have experienced the jealousy of Saul, the persecution of the enemy, and only glimpses of promise. What you cannot see is the soft pliability of your heart, allowing Me to mold you into your future destiny. Deep places in your heart have pondered if there a future in your call. You have even come into agreement with the other voices that say, "This is it."*

*Not so. I AM has released a roar announcing your identity and purpose. I have released the sound of who you are into the earth. Just as Joseph spent the last two years in seclusion, he was suddenly summoned to the courts of influence. Today is your "suddenly." You call it the "beyond thinking factor." I call it another day in the office. Watch Me as I begin the countdown. Watch how I will maneuver every circumstance, every intersection, every divine appointment, and every cry of your heart. I AM weaving them all together into a cord of many strands that will not be broken. I AM deploying your appointment with complete deliverance now. Not tomorrow—today.*

*What do you say? We can do this together, and you will learn the true definition of marvel. Marvel because I AM marvelous.*

### Show Me "Marvelous"

I am a chosen generation, a royal priesthood, a holy nation. I am one of Your own special people who proclaims the praises of my God who called me out of darkness and into Your marvelous light. Thank

You, Father, for Your call on my life. I commit to grow into it despite the battles with my flesh. I may stumble and fall in this area at times, but I cannot be apart from Your presence because I am seated with You. If I am seated with You, I am in a place of victory and destiny. It is here, when I am at my most vulnerable, that I am hidden under Your wings. I cannot be separated from Your presence or from my purpose. Show me "marvelous."

## For Reflection

1. Have you found yourself in the middle of a training exercise in which God has allowed difficulties and challenges to mold you into a vessel of honor? Discover who God is for you in the middle of these situations. Ask Him who He wants to be for you.
2. Do you believe God can release a "suddenly" into your circumstances? Can you be content with that knowledge?
3. Redefine the word marvelous as it describes God's heart for you.

# 10

# *Dancing on the Waters of Yesterday's Limitations*

## The Light of the World Is in Me

I have Your light in me, and wherever I go and whatever I do, that light is fixed on my talents, time, and treasure. Your light attracts others. Darkness is dispelled by the penetrating beams of Your presence from within me. I am a lighthouse full of Your goodness, kindness, and compassion.

I have a guarantee, a covenant certainty, that I will never grope in darkness because the light of Christ within me is everlasting. Your light makes me unafraid of evil tidings. It guards my heart as I grow in trust in You. Shine on my enemies. I will not be satisfied until the enemies of my destiny are blinded and defeated. For those positioned to fight against Your purposes in me, arrest any noncompliance and loose the purpose and destiny of Your Kingdom within me. Dispel the strongholds of darkness within my sphere of authority with the blinding light of Your glory.

How can I be overwhelmed when You are Captain of my ship? I can sail the high seas of this life encouraged and excited. You are teaching me how to rest and trust in the midst of stormy conditions. In the past I have permitted the storms to shipwreck me from Your destination. You intend every storm, I have learned, to bring me closer to my purpose.

You are teaching me how to take every problem, stress, and anxiety into the deep waters and drown them. There must be a problem in order to activate Your promise. Problems are designed to sever my dependence on the shore, washing me into the deep places of trust in You. It is here that I see how marvelous the mind of Christ is. Every storm is filled with opportunities for me to grow in my identity and be released in my promise. Develop within me the capacity to live in the understanding of Your limitless power. You are full of possibilities.

Prepare the way that I take and align me with my divine purpose. I surrender all of me to all of You. Pour out Your best for me. I need Your affirmation. Shield me today, Lord. Commission my life as an offering to others. Pour me out and refill me to overflowing in the constant waterfall of Your precious thoughts and intentions over me. While I am being poured out as Your offering, the opinions and favor of man become unimportant. You cause everyone to serve Your purpose in me, and I am honored to be Your gift to others. You are greatly exalted.

## Go Deep for Destiny

*Good morning, son. I have been waiting for you. I have much to say to you that will calm your fears and anxieties. I AM peace. I AM rest. I AM wisdom, understanding, and strength. Try to see Me in the beauty of who I AM without getting stuck in what I can do. I can do everything. But when you operate in a narrow perception of Me, you cannot see the vastness of My greatness. Greatness is My character. My great deeds and actions come directly from My character.*

*Get to know Me and launch out from your shallow shoreline. Traverse the deep waters of My fullness. Be impressed at what I can do, but be astonished by who I AM. I AM the amazing God, singing and dancing over you. If you will come up higher to that clear glass dance floor just above you, you will recognize that I have been waiting to sing and dance with you. When You and I dance closely and you hear the soft whisper of My love, you will begin to receive the fullness of understanding and wisdom.*

*The vastness of My love and care has become your anchor, and your thoughts toward Me lift the sails high to catch the wind of My Spirit. When you struggle and get bogged down in your journey, it is not because I AM withholding My grace and blessing. When you battle the fears, inhibitions, and weak places that defined you in your past, I take that opportunity to cast you back upon My potter's wheel, reforming and reshaping your past identity into My perceptions of You.*

*Your vulnerable moments are the very atoms and molecules of the waves on the sea that await your footprint. Master them by allowing Me to be the Master Teacher and releaser of destiny. It is out here. Your destiny awaits you, beloved, in the deep places. Instead of looking at a difficulty as something that drowns your purpose, look at each challenge as another wave of My glory bringing you safely to Me. Enjoy these moments and do not be fearful; be delighted in Me. Be overwhelmingly and carelessly confident in Me. I will guide you through each difficulty with favor, influence, and victory.*

*You bring much guilt and condemnation on yourself because you are gauging your performance on your past perceptions. Do not worry. I am your future and I determine your coming and going. I brought you into the deep water of change, not to drown you but to douse you with persona. Every step you take outside the boat of your comfort on the deep waters of your tomorrow will take you into your future. Let's have fun together as we walk hand in hand. I will never leave your side. I have deployed all of heaven on your behalf. Cast your pearls at the feet of those I direct toward you.*

*Remember, deep cries unto deep. I do not reside in the shallows of your thinking anymore. That is only My reflection. Come up higher, face to face with Me. You are Mine and I am yours. I chose you first, son. You will always be Mine.*

## For Reflection

1. How can you express God's goodness, kindness, and compassion in the sphere of your influence?
2. Are storms in life positive or negative? What do you consider the purpose of a storm? What can you learn from it?
3. Because God is the Captain of your ship, who is responsible for the storms in your life? How does that change your response to them?

# 11

# See Things from My Perspective

## Old Man Overboard

I am seeing new horizons in my relationship with You. As I sit with You in heavenly places, I can see with a wider perspective. From up here, I easily recognize the baggage of my past that I have tried to carry into this new place. I clearly see the old, poor perception of myself, my inadequacies, and the hurt and pain from the last season. Every piece of this negative baggage is old, worn, and unattractive. I take each one into the deep waters of the river of life with You and drown it.

I have chosen to walk in my freedom. Up here I put on the beautiful mind of Christ, in which You whisper who I am, while my faulty misperceptions of identity sink deeper and deeper out of sight. I am free from the power of the memory of every offense—even those memories I have suppressed deep within. I push them over the edge of the boat and into the depths of the water below, never to surface again. About all my striving and futile efforts to be recognized or affirmed, controlled by the opinions of man, I quickly acclaim, "Old man overboard."

From up here I hear the gentle words of the Holy Spirit asking for the opportunity to implant His full influence in my life. Yes, Father, yes, yes, yes. Work out Your powerful intentions in me by replacing this vacuum with the fullness of Your Holy Spirit. Sweep my house clean. I invite You permanently to live in me. My boat has crossed the equator of surrender, and I am all in. I speak to my new man to arise as I run to You. My new beginnings have been activated in the new man as I stand in Your pool of refreshing. I have lightened my ship by tossing overboard the baggage of yesterday. Now, Holy Spirit, come and fill this temple.

## An Epic Adventure

*I have reserved seating for you to see the epic adventure of your life from a higher perspective. It is the place where you are seated with Christ in every situation. It is up here that you hear the language of your true identity. I crown you with confidence—not the kind that you conjure up through faith, but true statements of who you are from My heart. You have to come up higher to hear My words. As I speak your beautiful persona over you from this high place, you are in a position to become a triumphant overcomer fighting from the place of victory. You have only to receive.*

*Your ship was loaded down with trinkets from yesterday, weighed down by past failures, hurts, and negative personality traits formed through the course of your lifetime. Allow Me to take them all and drown them in the deep waters of forgetfulness. Release them and give them to Me. As you do, I AM refilling this void with the mighty Holy Spirit to impart your persona. Your new identity is being announced, and the valuables of yesterday will seem worthless in the light of My new glory and favor.*

*You are now living an ascended lifestyle residing in the high place with Me, where all that I have is yours. I AM hiding you in My Son and you are hidden in Me. Enjoy this secret place, this habitation where the cares of life and human efforts to overcome are futile. Revelation is available from this high place that overcomes everything victoriously and triumphantly. Speak the language of heaven to open up the portals to My powerful presence to transform and transfigure the earth.*

*I have appointed you as a director of heaven on earth. I have established your credentials. Declare war on all your negative behavior with the newness of life that comes only from being positioned in the high place of the beautiful mind of Christ. Let's go to work together from up here.*

## For Reflection

1. What things in your life do you want to throw overboard?
2. If you were able to see this process from the heavenly places, and you were able to see yourself in the boat of your past identity, describe what you would see from this heavenly perspective.
3. Ask the Holy Spirit to fill those vacated areas with His great intentions toward you. Begin a conversation with Him about them.

# 12

## A New Dance

### Set Free and Sent Forth

Thank You for wisdom. Whenever I wander off or become lazy or careless, Your wisdom calls out to me. When I respond to Your wisdom, I align myself under the spout of Your release. Your Spirit pours over me and brings me back to the safety of Your loving intentions. You are pouring out Your grace and mercy continuously, and I must position myself to receive them.

I am free, Father, from shame and condemnation. I cannot see them any longer, for the drenching rain of Your Spirit has washed them away. This brings me to a new place in our relationship. I want to experience more of You. You have been busy rearranging my life, my priorities, and my passions. Pull out the things in me that do not mix with Your outpouring. Thank You for washing me clean from the memories of yesterday's bondage and hindrances.

Your promises are surety. I count on Your Word. It speaks of Your character and heart for the broken, and it reveals the truth of Your overwhelming desire to bless all who will turn toward You. I see You face to face today, knowing I have been positioned for this time. You place me in pastures of compassion and encouragement for others, and release resources and redemption through me. I am here for such a time as this. Never let me miss my mark in history. Enlarge my heart to reflect Yours in large, open places.

I take You into the mountains of education, family, religion, and government; into the mountains of the media, the arts and business; because there is a shift in the Spirit inside me. You are speaking, and my hearing is being fine-tuned to listen.

My number is about to be called. Announce my number and release me into the destiny of my storyline. You have appointed me as a director of heaven on earth. I bring the Spirit of life and resurrection into those dead, cursed places that have tolerated the bondage of Egypt. No longer will I be overwhelmed by the appearance of the impossibilities that linger in the heights of the massive mountains before me. No longer will I worry about performance-based days, equating these with value or accomplishment. I walk on the waters of impossibility. It is not by might, nor by power, but by Your Spirit that I am able, and I declare that I am well able.

## Dance on the Waters with Me

*What pleasure you bring to My heart! You are learning to surrender the old ways and thoughts to new man thinking. Old is old, and it is on its way out. New is new, and it will cover the earth. Old does not work in this new day. You cannot use yesterday's war strategies to target today's battles. You are in a different season with a more difficult degree of challenge. You are also in a day with greater revelation, power, and authority available. Cross the threshold that separates the old from the new. Enter into the best I have for you. I AM placing your greatest battles ahead of you. I have called you for such a time as this. Say goodbye to the old. The old way of doing things is a hindrance to the new. Ask Me to show you the new way.*

*The old way of repetitive mistakes no longer controls you. Your upgraded understanding of My grace is much more than a ticket into heaven; it is a new river of discovery awaiting you. The old cannot experience the depths of this understanding; it can only stay afloat here in its boat of limitations. The new understanding of grace is a lifestyle of water-walking and water-dancing. Old thinking will keep you inside the boat. The manna season is over. Limitation is a lifestyle of the past. Every season of your life—every test, challenge, and opportunity—has been to prepare you for this very season of grace. The boat will not be able to navigate the waters ahead. Get out of the boat. It is time to walk and dance on the waters.*

*New means new. New is something you have never before experienced—new glory, new authority, new understanding, new conversations, new victories. Say goodbye to the old. Say goodbye to the dead; you have paid your last respects to it. I have already started the new thing in you. Fill My temple with the worship of a warrior ready for deployment. It is time to go nose to nose with every challenge. It is time to free the captives. It is time to liberate the lost. It is time to rise and fulfill your storyline.*

*Step out of your boat, quit listening to the dead corpses talking, and begin your journey on top of the water, not in it. Take My hand, and I will teach you to dance on the waters with Me. As we dance, you will begin to see yesterday's impossibilities dissolve into the sea of our dance. We are going to a place you have never been before. I have baited the enemy into this place. Little does he know that he is following you right into an ambush. Here I will pass judgment on him and release Mordecai promotions to My faithful.*

*So get out of the boat. Set your face like flint and dance on the waters with Me this very day as I lead.*

## For Reflection

1. What does greater revelation, power, and authority look like in your new way of thinking?
2. What are the impossibilities you see as immovable? What stands in the way of your stepping into your promise?
3. What do you see as the difference is between "walking" on water and "dancing" on it?

DAVE McDANIEL

# 13

## You Can Do This!

## What I Know

When I am overwhelmed, my heart cries out to You to lead me to the Rock, the sure foundation that is higher than I. I know that when the enemy comes in like a flood, You raise up a standard against him, making me more than a conqueror in Jesus. I know I am victorious in every situation. I know in whom I have believed, and am persuaded that You are able. I know You will keep me in perfect peace when my mind is stayed on You. I know that You are my refuge and my strength. I get it that the enemy wants to challenge Your word, promise, and inheritance to me.

Get me off this merry-go-round of the same scenery, the same emotional vulnerabilities, and the same shipwreck of feeble-mindedness. When I don't know what to do or say, I turn my mind toward Your thoughts of me. Good thoughts! Great plans!

## Yesterday Is Gone

*If there is a mountain before you, apply My grace to that mountain. I do not hold you accountable to your past because I AM a present-future God. Nothing from yesterday has a legal hold on you unless you allow your mind to surrender permission. I remember your development from yesterday, but I do not remember your past sin, failures, and shortcomings because they are under the blood of Jesus. I see you differently than you see yourself. You are eyeing your challenges according to yesterday's confidence, and that will torment you.*

*Do not measure today's pressures of performance against yesterday's talents and abilities. Yesterday you did not understand the fullness of being an overcomer; today you do. Yesterday you could not do what presently lies before you; today you can. Yesterday's understanding and wisdom were lacking and incapable of addressing your present; today I AM here, and I have promised to be with you in everything. I have promised to enlarge you and stretch you into uncomfortable places of growth necessary to give birth to the harvest of your future. I will lead you triumphantly into this new place.*

## For Reflection

1. What are the differences between the responses of your old nature and your new one to something overwhelming?
2. Along this journey of growth, do you see yourself the same way God sees you? How does God see you?

# 14

# Turning the Tables in Your Favor

## Staking the Kingdom Flag of Enough!

You see me and hear me. You are close to my broken heart. But Father, I no longer want to be one who cries out from a state of helplessness. That comes from an earthly perspective of identity. I want to be in such intimate relationship with You, living from a higher position seated with You, that the arrows of fear and intimidation cannot reach me. Instead of crying out for deliverance, my only cries are "Holy, holy, holy."

Rarely do troubles, fears, and intimidation have anything to do with me. As I endure these, eternal seeds of the Kingdom are planted and the territory staked. That is what the battle is about. In my position seated in heavenly places in Christ Jesus, I hover over the bounty of my territory and inheritance that lies beneath. When the time arrives that Your Kingdom purpose has been planted in its entirety, every single affliction I have encountered will have served its purpose, and You will stake the ground with my Kingdom flag of *Enough!* All fears, intimidating voices, accusations, and limitations will scurry to the place of my next miracle, and I will begin the process of taking territory all over again.

There is no retreat or flight backward. There is not even a standstill position that awaits reinforcements. This is a constant, unperceived, and gradual taking of territory right from underneath the enemy's nose. When he finally realizes that the shaking he is experiencing is the foundation of Your glory taking the ground underneath him, he has no choice but to flee, and the angel of the Lord laughs in delight. You and I can play the game each time with him: "Now you see me, now you don't."

## Watching the Enemy Flee

*I like that. By remaining in the abiding place of My protective presence, you are delivered from all your fears. You operate in confidence.*

*Your mission is implemented by steadfastness and steadiness. I control the direction and the speed. You are with Me. There will be times when you and I proclaim the word of My intentionality directly into the face of the enemy, and suddenly he will look around frantically and not be able to find us.*

*He tries to do the same thing to you. He constantly looks for openings to sow fear and intimidation, but it cannot work against you. Your stare of confidence in Me intimidates him. That same fear and intimidation he sought to sow boomerangs back on him, and he becomes terrified. Our position is hidden from the enemy. He will see us, and then instantly he will not be able to find us.*

*But I know where he is. I AM commissioning My children to take the territory of darkness. I know where the enemy is hiding, and I see the territory he is fighting to maintain. In this hour, I AM releasing the coordinates of victory, and all you have to do is go forward and be the carrier of My presence in this dark place. I will do the rest. He will see us coming, and we will see him fleeing.*

## For Reflection

1. Read Ephesians 2:5–6. Is sitting with Christ Jesus in heavenly places an issue of performance or placement?
2. What are the advantages of being seated in heavenly places in Christ Jesus?
3. Have you decided once and for all to stake the Kingdom flag of *Enough*! and take your rightful place in Him? The circumstances may remain the same, but what happens to your perspective of them from this position?

# 15

# Vertical Positioning for Horizontal Purpose

## Newer Heights of Understanding

I pray that You will be the exceedingly "beyond thinking" factor in my life right now (Ephesians 3:20). There is such a hidden passion unbridled in me. You created me with a specific identity to fulfill.

When I feel overwhelmed, be my refuge and hiding place. You are the keeper, my Shepherd, and the protector of Your own. Show me what is missing in my relationship with You. Help me forgive myself for all the mistakes of the past. It is a new day. Elevate me higher into an ascended lifestyle of knowing You as Savior and Friend. Everything is in Your hands, and I am learning to rest in my position in You. Renew my thinking with the thoughts that You are having about me and destroy the reproach of my past.

You chose me, Father. Replace my dead-end life with the resurrection power of the new life. Teach me to embrace my newness of life. Bring me into relationship with You so we can work together on areas of my life that are not working. I gladly lay aside the old self and renew my mind in who You say I am. I willingly lay down the old and renew my mind to focus on who I really am—a new creation in You. Bring my mind into agreement with Yours. It is a progressive learning experience that I may become the embodiment of Your every thought toward me.

Teach me Your righteousness in this place. I enter this beautiful place of exploration and discovery as You determine every step for me. I rest in Your faithfulness to accomplish this in me, and I come into agreement that this is the first day of my new life.

## Grab the New

*Enjoy this eternal process where the richness of your life exceeds all expectations. You are made rich by being made new. Everything else will become life-draining to you. Only the new life begets a new life. This is the new place of My life-giving rivers.*

*New, new, new ... you have entered through the door of this newest and most rewarding season of revival. You are that revival. The old cannot survive the altitude of higher thinking. I have opened the door separating the old from the new. Do not worry about how to discard the old; it will die for lack of oxygen in the higher elevations I AM taking you to. The newness of My life will ground all heaviness and gravitational pulls of the old. I AM propelling you like an Apollo spacecraft into the higher atmosphere, where it must discard the extra weight that got it there.*

*In the higher elevations, yesterday's anointing cannot serve today's purpose. You absorb the new through a change in the elevated atmosphere you have entered rather than by looking for ways to modify your behaviors. To come up higher means coming into agreement with how I see you, then stepping into the behaviors associated with it. The old self can navigate only on a horizontal plane. The new self, by contrast, is designed to develop through your vertical placement in Christ. You cannot go any higher than the heavenly places with Christ Jesus.*

*I call you higher than you have ever gone. How do you do this? Follow the inspiration of the Holy Spirit. To paraphrase Paul: "Just press on so that you may lay hold of that for which I have for you. Lay hold of Christ. Do not regard yourself as having laid hold of it yet; but do one thing: Forget what lies behind, reach forward to what lies ahead, and press on toward the goal for the prize of the upward call I have for you in Christ Jesus" (Philippians 3:12–14, NASB).*

*The sequence to come up higher is simple: Forget your past, reach forward, and grab onto your identity. Then press in to the purpose I have for you in this lifetime. Come up higher and soar in the heights of My best for you.*

## For Reflection

1. How should you respond when confronting difficult circumstances? Do you deal with them on a horizontal plane or on a vertical climb? What is the difference?
2. What are the three key action verbs in Philippians 3:12–14 that can help you live an ascended lifestyle rather than a horizontal existence?

# 16

## Dance on Your Problems

### No More Boats

Overshadow me with Your presence. You are my confidence and proficiency. My name has been changed and my purpose revealed. I dance with You on the waters of yesterday's impossibilities. No more holds, no more taunts, no more limitations. The fullness of Your presence has touched the soles of my feet. Deploy me into my purpose, Father. Territory, strategies, and wisdom are mine in You.

My faith is buoyed to rise with the level of the water. Take the boat from which I came and send it far away, never to return. No more boats, Lord. I want to step into my destiny and walk on water. Speak the miracle of exponential release from all limitation as I dance with You, Father, Son, and Holy Spirit. I stand on Your promises, provision, and purpose, ready to align myself to receive the fulfillment of my promises and prophetic words. My enemy is powerless here. You joyfully announce his demise as You sing out my identity. Make a public spectacle of him as You did Haman on his own gallows. The enemy placed gallows in my life to destroy my destiny, but instead they announce it! No more holds on my future unless it is Your hand on it.

You showered on me the former rain of anointing sufficient for my past. Now You are causing the former rain and the latter rain to come together in the first month, the time of new beginning. I can see the threshing floor filled with wheat and the vats overflowing with new wine and oil. This is my place, Lord. This is the floor set before me. You restore all that has been stolen; all the years the swarming locusts have eaten. I stand in a position of infinite possibility. You have dealt wondrously with me, and I will never be put to shame.

## For Reflection

1. What does "dancing on the waters with Jesus" mean to you in your current situations in life?
2. What is the purpose of the merging of the former and latter rain? What is your part in this? His part?

# 17

# *The Power of Our Dance*

## Captured By Your Presence

I have felt the shift of Your commission and the entrance of Your awesome authority and glory. You have brought me to Your banqueting table. I am strengthened and launched into my destiny as Your voice calls my name. Increase my understanding of the mysteries of Your heart. Soak me in truth and protect me with Your intentionality. This is not a season for my mind to chase after whims or wants, but to chase the knowledge of God. Teach me, Father, and impart to me the wisdom to rightly discern all things. I cannot renew my thinking without fresh water from the Holy Spirit to wash over me and regenerate me. I come and drink from Your never-ending fountain of living water. This is the place where I find rest through intimacy with You.

I love You so much, Lord. My heart cannot contain my passion for Your presence this morning. You have captured me. Never release me from this place. Only increase my capacity to receive more and more and more and more. Refills are free. I cannot dance on the waters unless You are there releasing more of You. Deep cries unto deep. Release the affections of Your heart to explode with mine. Bring cataclysmic changes to my thinking and piece together all the parts that have been separated from the whole, refined carefully and meticulously for such a time as this.

## The Awesome Place of My Permission

*Come and dance on the waters with Me. The freshness of My presence can be found on the waters surrounding you. I call every part of you I have been molding on My potter's wheel to come together and form the new you, the refined you. Do not fear the furious winds and waves. They are under My command and serve My purpose. I have created a glassed dance floor on the waters of impossibility. You cannot sink when you dance with Me. I will teach you how to dance the mountains of opposition down.*

*May I speak to you about the awesome place of My permission? All of Me in all of you releases the hasps that have been padlocked. The bars of iron will now become bars of righteousness. I have done something special today in the Spirit. An announcement from the corridors of My throne room has caused the sound of My intentions to reverberate throughout all of creation. I have proclaimed that the new beginning has now begun. Seasons upon seasons of preparation have been prerequisite for the new beginning of the story of who you were created to be, the purpose you have in the earth—and the joy that is so rich when your preparation meets at the intersection of surrender. Nothing can stop what I AM doing.*

## Deployed by My Sound

*Our dance has released a majestic sound from heaven that has sent the enemy scurrying to defeat. When the sound of majestic worship arises from those who know who they are in Christ, the result is confusion in the enemy's ear. Such resounding peals of majesty penetrate the tunnels of darkness like a fireball of praise ignited by jet fuel. The enemy is no match for those who have crossed over. He cannot attack your mind when you are residing in the mind of Christ. All sickness and disease, all lack and deficiency, all impossibilities and barriers have now served their purpose. The heat of majestic praise incinerates all that.*

*Commissioned are those who will be illustrations and carriers of My presence who will change the atmosphere by getting out of the boat and stepping onto the waters of yesterday's impossibilities. Come, dance with Me on the rivers of life. Yesterday's impossibilities have turned into today's opportunities. There is power in the dance. There is power released with each step to crush the lies of the past, the limitations of yesterday, and past seasons that have deceived you from your future.*

*The past is over. You have crossed the threshold of no return, and the wide-open vista before you, full of infinite possibility, is yours to explore. No more holds, no more taunts, no more limitations, for the water of My fullness has touched the soles of your feet, and you are complete in Me. I will flow over you with My river of life that will wash away the memories of your past. The season you have entered is the season of your purpose.*

*Just as troops are deployed with purpose and objectives after they complete seasons of military training, this very day I AM deploying you into your future. I AM giving you territory in the Spirit. I AM giving you clear strategies and abundant wisdom that you were never able to experience before. This happens out here on the waters. The only thing that can keep you from Your inheritance is to retreat to the boat from which you came.*

*Once you have tasted what is in store, you will be impassioned for more, never again satisfied by a drink from the old well. I AM the new well, and these rivers of living water are fresh and never recycled.*

## For Reflection

1. What does it mean to find rest through intimacy with God? What does that look like in your life?
2. Are there areas of your thinking that you would like to have upgraded to fulfill your purpose? What are some of them?
3. What is your storyline? What is the divine life purpose for which you were created? What is keeping you from fulfilling that purpose?
4. How will you look at circumstances and challenges to your life purpose in light of God's invitation to dance on them?

# 18

## *Overflowing with New Wine*

### May I Have This Dance?

Your presence this morning is amazing. You were waiting for me today because You have so many things You want to say to me. I want to hear them all. I have stepped through the door into my purpose and Your passion. My chest is exploding with Your glorious presence. I bow down. I honor You, Lord. I love You. I sense such beauty, peace, and majesty all at the same time. My tears wash Your feet, and I am like a new wineskin thirsty for fullness. I kiss Your feet with a submitted body, soul, and spirit that rise into alignment with my position before You. I release my song—dance music for us. You lead the dance. Everything else has bowed its knee to the fire of Your presence.

I feel free and light on my feet. You have taken and removed all reproach from the past. You are a present-future God, and I want only what You want. I want to think only what You think. I want to say only what You are saying. I want to become only what and who You say I am. Lead me into the green pastures of fellowship with You. Take me into triumph and my rehearsal of who I am becoming. Surround me with people of anointing who can escort me safely into this place.

### New Wine for New Wineskins

*What an amazing work Holy Spirit is doing. He is moving quickly, empowered by excitement and anticipation at how you will react and respond when you see what I have ordered for you. He's that way. He is full of excitement and power for you because you have turned your affections toward Me. Face to face and cheek to cheek with Me causes Him to accelerate a release of glory, releasing it on those new wineskins that can house the new wine. He is not pouring it out in measure. He is not just filling it to the brim. He is pouring out the overflowing presence of My Spirit that looks like a fountain spring exploding with the sound of My glory.*

*Your past-present mocks and taunts your persona. My responding glory incinerates the last chapters of your life that have no connection to you here. I AM teaching you how to walk into your future by permitting those distant sounds of the past to remind you of the places from which you came. You will never be satisfied with old wine thinking and living again. Such glory is before you. Holy Spirit is your Friend and Guide, desiring to put you on His back like a backpack to carry you on this journey.*

## For Reflection

1. What is your song to the Lord?
2. Have you offered up the old wineskin for a new one? Who is the Holy Spirit to you? Ask Him to reveal Himself to you and fill up your new wineskin with the presence of God. Has this changed your song to the Lord?

# 19

## Heaven's Mathematics

### From This Day Forward, I Will Bless You

Father, prepare me for this leg of my journey. Cultivate the soil inside me. Break open every inch of fallow ground that would harden me from experiencing my purpose. You are the righteous Judge and merciful Father who knows timing. The danger in knowing my future is that I want to shortcut and operate from that place now. But I do not want to miss anything You have for me. I leave the timing to You. All the prayers and tears I have deposited with You have been planted.

You told me to consider the seed in the barn, and then You said, "from this day forward, I will bless you" (Haggai 2:18-19, NKJV). I have been transformed by that word. Every blessing, every release of anointing, every word of encouragement, every nugget of revelation is seed in the barn. Show me the soil into which to plant this seed. Release anointing to destroy the works of darkness that have been hiding. Reestablish the strongholds of Kingdom authority in my regions of influence—in government, in people, in gender reconciliation, in finance, in ministry, in the marketplace—all in abundance. This is my inheritance, and it is mine in the Spirit.

Arise in me. Fit me on Your hand like a tight glove. It is time to release the power of my God. Jubilee is approaching. Destiny and purpose are moving in closely upon inheritance and freedom. As these two sets of desires from Your heart collide, I call forth the lightning and thunder of Your presence to announce their arrival.

Open my barn, Father, and commission the locked-up fruit to change the world. Teach me how to pray the prayer that Jesus prayed. Teach me how to pray the prayers of Your heart that determine the destinies of others.

### Multiplication, Not Addition

*The times and seasons are in My hand. I determine release, and I set the dates to release My children from the servitude of preparation from past seasons of life. Struggles were necessary to push you toward your future. Without them, your wings would not be strong enough to break through the cocoon of destiny. I have been at work changing your identity from a caterpillar to a butterfly. Your own persistence through the dissatisfaction of knowing there is more has pushed you to press forward. You realized there was no further life in the places of yesterday. You asked for more of Me and for the fulfillment of your purpose. My fingerprints have been all over your development, especially in your struggles. Those times have been important for you to develop the strength and determination to fly wonderfully and without boundaries.*

*Acceleration and purpose have intertwined to create an entrance through the door into your destiny. You are ready to stand on the battleground of this next level of your purpose. Here you will take even more territory as you recover all territory taken from you in the past. Multiplication is my mathematical property. I AM not adding, subtracting, or dividing. I AM multiplying. Your accelerated movement is not without direction. I have deployed angels to bring vision to you that allows split-second decisions to be made without breaking speed.*

*My multiplication is not rudimentary but exponential. Dreams that have taken long to be fulfilled will now take only days because I AM multiplying their value each time. I use every conflict and growth opportunity to propel you forward and upward. Remember the revelations I have given you in these times? Ask Me to speak through you, and you will collapse in amazement at what you will experience. Just go and be, and leave the rest to Me.*

## For Reflection

1. What prayers and tears have you deposited with the Father? Write them down.
2. What is God teaching you in the struggles about who He is for you?
3. Have you been waiting on God to answer instead of going forward and asking for His wisdom, strength, and revelation of how these struggles are developing something deep in you? How do struggles propel you forward into your destiny?

# 20

# *Focus on What I Have Spoken*

## Finding Delight in My Present Purpose

Father of my present and future, my soul is trapped. You are teaching me how to find delight in my circumstances. But something very powerful is pulling me. I am being pulled into my future but my present is holding onto me. Your promises surround me with echoes of resounding invitation. This is the year of rest from my enemies. Show me how to contend for my future. Show me what You want to develop in me that is lacking for this next phase of our journey. Show me Your powerful faithfulness that eradicates despair and a weary heart.

From this day forward, I will bless you. That's Your word to me, Lord. All my promises are loaded onto the debit card of my future, and I have been created for this moment. My future is activated and ready to use. Show me what is missing from my relationship with You. What used to satisfy me is losing its hold on me. I have been secluded in an appointed place to separate the passions of my past from those needed for my future. My eyes can see more clearly, and my ears are more attuned. The discomfort of the past with its sharp, jagged pokes has caused me to be restless and to flutter my wings. I have searched for escape and consolation. My future calls while my present is screaming.

Release the hold on my future by reaching down into the thicket and tenderly holding this wounded lamb. Nurse me to the healthy disposition of identity that develops the strength, stamina, and strong foundation that can carry the weight of Your glory on my future. Yet I must exercise patience and find delight in my present purpose. I must finish strong in this race first. Your covenant with me and the words You have spoken over me the past few months—I need to rehearse these. In them I will find delight in where I have been placed.

## Understand My Faithfulness

*What is frustrating you right now comes from a childish area in need of transformation. When I said that I could not show My disciples what I desired to show them, it was because they were not fully developed in their souls. If I had answered their prayers and revealed their futures, they would have been crushed. I want you, instead of asking for a revelation of the future, to see the many places along the way to your promise. I want you to encourage yourself in Me and be excited in our plans together. Develop such a close and trusting relationship with Me that I can reveal My plans to you in secret, earmarked for specific times. These are conversations of trust.*

*By the way, you have allowed two interruptions to occur while I AM speaking. Do you not see? There is a renewing of your mind needed to press into what I AM saying without being distracted. I AM releasing stability in your mind, for I AM your delight. I have chosen this specific time and these appointed people in your life. Will you press into Me as your delight, or will you chase reprieve from these temporary afflictions?*

*Instead of searching for escape, search for who I AM for you in these times. It will develop more patience in you and endurance needed for the trip ahead. Be encouraged, son, for the great I AM is with you to guide you into this "can't miss" future. Guard your heart and see things from My perspective. Find your delight in this.*

## For Reflection

1. "From this day forward, I will bless you." How can you use this powerful promise as a weapon in your life?
2. "I want you, instead of asking for a revelation of the future, to see the many places along the way to your promise." In what ways does this change your thinking about the journey ahead?

# 21

# *The Stage Has Been Set*

## My Confidence Is in You

"Blessed be the God and Father of our Lord Jesus Christ, who has blessed us with every spiritual blessing in the heavenly places in Christ" (Ephesians 1:3, NKJV). It is time to wade from the shallows and launch into the deep. As I submit myself to You this morning and allow Your redemptive power to change and transform me, my body is being transformed. My back has been spasming and hurting, but as I sit here in Your presence, I am conscious of Your Spirit healing me right now! The enemy accuses, but I stand in the deep places of trust. It is not medication but the radiation of Your presence that heals me. Thank You, Lord.

I am meditating on past testimonies of Your character in the Word that I have found to be true through my own personal experiences. This is a time of supernatural favor and deliverance, a great time in You. The testimonies of Your deliverance cause me to soar. Just as Gideon tore down his father's idol and was threatened as a result (Judges 6:25–31), my abilities and calling have found opposition from some of those around me. But I am moving from gleaning what has been left behind to reaping what has been purposed and prepared for me in this place.

My confidence is in You. You are my refuge, my light, my provider. You are mine and I am Yours. You are my strength, peace, comfort. You are the great I AM. Open my eyes to see clearly in the days ahead. Increase my passion and sustain my strength for this new place of favor. I am healed in this place—physically, emotionally, spiritually, financially. I am created for this time to have an answer, a solution, as the earth is shaking around me. I have been chosen as one of those to confront the enemy. I am created to have a voice for such a time as this. That is who I am. Every problem, every deadline is an opportunity to display excellence. Give me the voice and the confidence to go forward.

## Showtime!

*Say goodbye to the things that held you back yesterday. The sunset of yesterday has given birth to the dawning of a new day and a season of unthinkable possibilities. What you call the "beyond thinking" factor I call another day at the office. These times are reserved for you as this crossroad beckons you to cross over.*

*I can stop time and I can accelerate it. Time will serve My purpose for you. As you embrace the excitement and intention I have for you over these next several days, continue to journal My goodness and kindness. This will be the basis for a new thing I AM writing on the tablet of your heart.*

*You are to share these things. Pay attention. Do not be governed by the first responses of your emotions. Be obedient to the call, and you will thrash through what used to be considered places of hard treading and minimal gleaning. Beginning right here, right now, you will go through these hard places plowing the fallow ground with the penetrating revelation of heaven. I will burn up all things that do not serve My purpose for you. It is showtime! Every day will appear like a Christmas celebration of giving and receiving. Listen and watch. I have declared and therefore it is. Stand up and be counted. Step out and be rewarded. Show up to every fight in the power of My might. Seize every opportunity. Great changes have been preordered and paid in full.*

## For Reflection

1. Do you need healing in your life? As you read this entry, personalize it. Receive the healing for your need through the anointing and declaring of these words. Apply them and receive your healing. Sit in His presence and worship Him.

2. What are some examples of God's goodness and kindness to you? Write them down and read them to the Father.

# 22

## Enjoy the Process

### Higher and Deeper through Process

You are taking me higher and higher in Your glory. Now take me deeper and deeper in my pursuit of fullness. The very covenant You have released has become the path on which I travel. Your covenant is not just an end result of blessing and promise; it is also the rich process in getting there. It points the way to the promise, and it becomes the scenery and intersecting points along the way. Open my mind to understand covenant. I have embraced only the superficial meaning of this great agreement.

I have looked for the fulfillment of Your Word while attempting to ignore the circumstances around me. How do my current circumstances, distractions, and confrontations fit into Your covenant blessing? Joseph's circumstances served his purpose, and all of Egypt was transformed. Paul and Silas worshiped their way through their circumstances and brought in the Kingdom of salvation. Harvest resulted. Circumstances didn't change because Paul and Silas had a word from You. Instead circumstances bowed the knee to serve the purpose of God. Your greatness became a testimony of Your deliverance to all, especially to the Philippian jailer.

You are always at work on my behalf. Your covenant is forthcoming. It is intertwined in my every breath and step. This means my circumstances are opportunistic. Great veins of gold and silver are awaiting, hidden inside every detail I come across. The richness of Your Kingdom is crying out from the broken, searching for purpose and identity. Your covenant crowns me with authority to declare and call forth Your purposes in the broken. I am a bright light dispelling the stronghold of darkness simply by stepping into my day. I encourage myself in You. Only You can guarantee my steps.

# Everything Serves Your Purpose

*The announcement of your future in the face of your present brings automatic conflict in the spirit realm of darkness. You do not see the fight taking place in the heavenly realm over your future. You are a key that unlocks generations and nations. The fight over territory has begun. You are facing a backlash of people and circumstances that do not understand their participation or their purpose.*

*The enemy's participation in this transition of your identity is a full onslaught against your soul. He cannot touch your spirit. I have placed protection around you. He can only release the noise of lies and intimidation, much as Goliath did. Why didn't Goliath just come into the camp of My army? He knew better. It is easy to intimidate from a distance when those darts can hit fearful places that paralyze you. But today I AM raising you up to meet this enemy face to face. Silence your soul with upgraded confidence in Me. I AM.*

*Do not fear the unknown, much of which will never materialize. Know this, beloved: My promises and declarations to bless you are not contingent upon your cautious or spontaneous decisions. That would make you a god. My word is eternal, and when I speak, there is a "Let there be" sound that rumbles across eternity. I do not retract My word: I act on it. Your future is not determined by your decisions when you are led by My Spirit. I have already penned these moments for their appropriate time. The taunts of the enemy produce a bloviating noise that keeps you from listening to My declarations over you. But I say, Arise in the confidence of My future over you.*

*Do you feel your strength being renewed in our time together? Encourage yourself in Me, and mute the noise around you. I control the hearts of the kings and queens of this world to do My bidding. Follow your heart and not your head. I AM with you. Don't cling to old security blankets. What I have spoken cannot be reversed. Be caught up in the majesty of that truth. Do not be swayed by the breeze but moved by the wind of the Spirit. Listen. You will hear the sound of My blessing inside the storm clouds of My rain over you. I AM storming over the earth, shaking the atmosphere, aligning everything according to the accelerated desires of My heart.*

## Smile

Father, be my delight and the only source of my strength and resources. Release the favor of Your blessing through the channels of my enemy, just like the destruction of Haman, and establish the gallows for every enemy that shakes a fist at Your purpose. Your Kingdom come, Your will be done, here in my life just as in heaven's declarations. I declare my favor from Your heart, Father God. Break open the skies of Your glory and empower me, that I may bring honor and glory to Your name.

## For Reflection

1. How do your current circumstances, distractions, and confrontations fit into God's covenant blessing for you?
2. How can you rest in the midst of a battle? Have you been able to smile in the midst of a battle? If not, why not?

# 23

# *I AM Fights Your Battles*

## Kingdom Principles of Warfare

*Your past, present, and future are not separated by time; they are separated by growth. When I bring you into promise, it is because you have addressed areas of growth in your understanding that can safely ensure your arrival and stay. I love you too much to allow blessing and favor on you if you have not established a foundation of honor in your life to carry the weight of My glory. Each day when you persevere through the difficulties by seeing Me in the midst of them, you begin to soar over those circumstances.*

*Whenever you are confronted by issues, do not be drawn into a fight I have not sanctioned. Many times My kids fight every evil spirit that taunts them. Even though you walk in authority to win every fight against them, you do not have the time. During this time of acceleration, the enemy cannot go at the speed we are going. Do not be slowed down by getting involved in fights that do not belong to you. The battles belong to Me. Some fights are nonviolent and a waste of energy.*

*Just because you see the enemy at work against you doesn't mean you have to fight him on his level. Instead, come higher in your relationship with Me. It is a place he cannot enter—one reserved only for you and Me. It is from this place that I will make a public spectacle of him. Being seated in higher elevations allows you to enjoy the fight from My perspective. This is what I mean by fighting from a place of victory, never toward it.*

*My intentions toward you are full of beauty and majesty, pregnant with blessing and fruitfulness—up here. These intentions are not meant to come down; you are meant to come up to meet them. I have spoken that you might remember this today. No longer do I breathe on you. I breathe through you.*

## For Reflection

1. What are the Kingdom principles of warfare over your identity? What part is yours and what part is God's?
2. What does it mean to you to fight from a place of victory rather than toward it? How do your perspective and language have to change?

# 24

## *Mission Possible*

### I Can Rest in War

You are teaching me how to be triumphant from a place of rest. I have become a vessel of rest in the midst of war. Resting in Your faithfulness and trustworthiness within stormy surroundings has caused me to see clearly from inside the eye of the storm and not from the surrounding whirlwinds. I can see from the calm place, the still waters, the green pastures, where the beauty of Your presence dwells. No longer am I searching for Your presence in the middle of the chaos. This is the place where I live, safe in the restful, peaceful eye of the storm. I find my rest and reward here. It is the place where I cannot miss receiving Your best for me.

When I learned yesterday that my plans for the future were at risk, I did not default to the former place of panic or intercession. I received the news from a place of rest and confidence, knowing that everything I experience serves Your purposes for me. Knowing that You are not a God of retreat but the One who is progressive in faithfulness and reward, I am excited to receive the blessing that has been reserved and multiplied by this very conflict. This is where my rest finds peace. My confidence is soothed and strengthened here.

There are benefits to my abiding in our secret place together. I fear nothing here. I am not intimidated here. I can hear only faintly the threats and accusations from the cheap seats. A protective shield surrounds the wide-open place where I dwell with You. It keeps me inside of You and distances the mocking and taunts from any other influence. I am not putting my head in the sand, trying to ignore an obvious situation. I am putting my head on Your heart, surrounded by Your arms, recognizing the safety of Your presence.

I can change the world I live from right here. It is the sweet place where the waterfalls of Your anointing and presence refresh me. When Your waterfalls roar over me, they deafen even the most remote sound from outside this place of refilling. My love and affection for You in this place continues to increase. It is here, Lord, where I live.

# Reward Right in Front of the Enemy

*I release a solid gold revelation for where* I AM *taking you. Morning upon morning of conversation and your pouring out your heart through honesty and childlike faith have expanded your strength and vision to receive My upgrades for this timely season. It is from these places that I have become your Shepherd. There is no lack in My presence, only abundance. When I send circumstances your way, they are never to hurt or destroy your confidence. Rather, their purpose is to make you lie down in the green grass where you learn to rest despite fearsome situations. From the green grass, there is plenty to receive.*

*I love to reward My children as the enemy watches. That is why I do it from this place. When I lead you, you are delivered into the serenity of still waters, bringing restored confidence in who* I AM *for you in this very circumstance. When your confidence in Me grows, your desire to stay closer to Me drives the stakes of your dwelling deep into the ground. From this place, I can lead you down paths of righteousness that are surrounded by the rich treasures of reward and surprise.*

*Do you see the relationship here? When you begin to follow the paths of righteousness, instead of visiting them, I can lead you safely to the place of your destiny for My name's sake.* I AM *intentional in this place of My indulgence to bless you. It is here that you will never fear death or what man and his opinions can do to you. It is here that you can laugh at the accusations designed to bring fear and paralysis.*

*You are with Me! I do all things well. I infuriate the enemy by preparing you a banqueting table to feast on as I require him to watch. As he watches you feast in sweet fellowship with Me, he is reminded over and over how he separated himself from this glorious table. It's fun to watch him huff and puff. One look from My eye, however, causes him to bow. In this place, one look from your eye will cause him to do the same thing. He is frightened of Jesus in you as you both are wrapped safely within Me.*

*When you understand this identity and placement, you live above the circumstances by walking on them hand in hand with Me, enjoying the bounty of the untried, ignoring the noise and listening to the sound of heaven. My goodness and mercy are your sentries that follow My presence, sealing what I have done in your life and freeing you to stay focused on your future. All is protected safely by My banner of love over you—undeniable, irrefutable, and unchangeable. Done deal. You have stepped with Me into the most bountiful place imaginable.*

*Release Kingdom and presence through the resources of your hands that I give you. One act of kindness and goodness will be multiplied into several, and the multiplication of My Kingdom will be released through it all.*

## What Does Abundance Look Like?

*In order to live an abundant life, you must live in the abundance of My presence. Instead of living from a reactionary mindset, responding to the demands of life, you operate from a proactive position. Here I call you to look at life through the lens of intimacy and deeper relationship with Me. Instead of being controlled by the pressures of financial challenges, or the diet and health of your body, or time restraints and job conflicts, you can cause these things to bow their knee to Jesus in you. How? Through living in the abundance of My presence. It is here that I have many things to tell you and teach you along the way. I will release wisdom and revelation in the knowledge of Me, and understanding to apply spiritual principles to the challenges here on earth.*

*Prioritizing your life in terms of what is most important indicates what is most valuable to you. Do not confuse activity with Me as being inactive elsewhere. The daily solitude of our fellowship is critical, but I call you to live your life by exhibiting and living out the product of our intimacy. During the night, I AM downloading untapped revelation, yours to explore with Me the next morning. As you do this more and more, a new lifestyle of intimacy forms, and you will live your life from this place and not toward it.*

*When you open up your day in conversation with Me, out of you will flow rivers of living water reserved for your day. Abundant life can only be an outflow of the abundance of life within. Each morning of solitude-abiding engages the power of the Holy Spirit inside you. I want to transform the atmosphere around you, and I operate best through open and willing vessels of surrender living out of the abundance of intimacy.*

*There is so much more to explore than what you have experienced. Each day you are growing more and more like Me. Never stop. Increase your time and attention to what is most important, and you will find what you are seeking—more of Me.*

## Captured by Your Heart

Father, I never want to live in a place outside of intimacy with You. I have been captured by Your heart, and cannot be satisfied with our close experiences of the past. The more I drink, the thirstier I become. You are intoxicating, Father, because You are so good. So kind and patient.

I can't help it, Father. It makes me weep every time I ponder just how good You are to me. I love You so much. I find myself growing closer and closer to You—maturation through saturation in Your presence—all because I want to. I cannot get enough of Your presence. The possibilities of my day expand proportionately with the level of my intimate fellowship with You.

Intimacy is not an event; it is my lifestyle. The quality of my performance is the outflow of my acquired closeness to Your heart. I don't want to limit myself to nuggets of wisdom and understanding. I want the mind of Christ and to operate in revelatory thinking, living out of wisdom and understanding. When I understand my placement of intimacy in You, my purpose, provision, and power become the byproduct.

## For Reflection

1. Read Psalm 23 and saturate yourself in its richness.
2. What enemies of your destiny must bow the knee to Jesus in you?
3. Discover the abundance of God's presence by intentionally pressing into the secret place with Him. Journal what that is like. Release your worship and the rights to yourself, and ask God to pour out the waterfall of His presence to transform you into His image.
4. How does maturation through saturation work? Remember, this is a journey, not a race. Enjoy the process.

# 25

## Appointing and Rehearsing the Prophetic

### A Supernatural Shaking

You are my source. My resources are heaven-sent and Father-protected. No matter how big the blessings become, all comes through Your hands. From this day forward, according to Haggai 2:18-19, I am blessed.

You exhort me in that same passage to consider the seed in the barn—meaning to appoint or rehearse. I have appointed every prophetic word and promise to be released and experienced. I practice the reality of these words as I move into their reality. Every word and promise stored in the storehouse has a time-release. If every promise and prophetic word were to be released all at once, I would easily be overwhelmed by Your goodness. You have built up a righteous expectation in me to receive Your goodness, to stand in my true identity to receive it, and to take it out into the earth and release it. My seed that is still in the barn has been earmarked for this time in history.

You are shaking the nations of the earth in two different ways. You are shaking the nations in the natural realm, and all the world's attention has been captured here. But the greater shaking is taking place in the spiritual realm, where You are causing a quivering in the hearts of the sons and daughters of God. It is a quivering, a glimmering like that of a calm sea that appears to be still. But beneath the surface, there is a shaking loose of the impossible; a liberation from the bonds of the past; an emancipation from the past into the present that is almost undetectable, yet certain.

The tsunami of Your Spirit is moving Your sons and daughters into oneness with You. This accelerated move is centering Your children in the middle of their life destiny. All this is happening even as the attention of the world is focused on the natural shaking taking place.

I wonder if that is what separated the great numbers of Gideon's original army from the remaining three hundred. The majority of the Body of Christ is caught up in the natural realm, while You are releasing fullness and splendor on those who have their ears to the ground, listening attentively to what the Spirit is saying. It doesn't make one more valuable than the other, but it does set apart those who can stand in this new place of identity and reward from those choosing to watch from a seat in the natural realm.

May I be so close to Your heartbeat and to the loving thoughts of Your mind toward me that I live in Your heart. I will no longer be a spectator but an active participant in shaping and transforming the earth into awakening spiritually to Your goodness. The shaking is the great spiritual awakening we have been waiting to experience.

It has shaken me, Father. I am no longer my own. I give You the reins of my life. Direct my every breath and thought into concert with Yours. I understand how the psalmist could say that his heart pants after You. My heart is so full toward You. Remove every element or distraction keeping me from truth and a deeper understanding of Your heart.

Wake up, soul, and pursue your purpose in God with vigor and desperation. No more emotional detours. There is no time. My eternal purpose is positioned before me, and I reach toward it with all my heart.

## For Reflection

1. To come into alignment to receive the fulfillment of a promise, we must rehearse that promise. How should your language, thinking, perceptions change in order to rehearse or appoint that word into action? Write it down and begin to rehearse it in front of the audience of your circumstances.

2. What seed have you sown into the barn of your future from which you are awaiting fruit to appear? How can your language, thinking, and perceptions change to prepare for this release? Begin to call forth your seed and fruitfulness in every circumstance. What would that look like?

# 26

## Overflowing Fullness

### Hearts of Abandonment

*As desperation for Me becomes your lifestyle, I also reach toward you with all My heart and attention. I have desired to draw you into a disciplined life for the journey ahead. I have scheduled a release of revelation and the fullness of My presence to those who run after Me with abandonment, pouring out their hearts and lives to others along the way. Scheduled. I have divine appointments scheduled to keep you overflowing in My fullness. Scheduled. I have every second of your life mapped out as My blueprint and prototype for the standard I AM raising up in the earth today.*

*You have fought well in past battles. Your placement in your job, church, and community has been to prepare you for something beyond. I have multiple purposes for every single action. While you have been faithful to stand in uncomfortable places, you have been planted as a standard against the enemy's assignment. You never had to take a swing or a swipe. You endured each day in strong prayer agreement with Me, recovering spiritual territory as a result. You take spiritual territory when you become the standard I raise by being steadfast in your position in the battle. The fight is Mine, and I never tire of being victorious.*

*Do not look at the natural conflicts surrounding you. Tap into the revelation and understanding of My heart for that place. I will show you how to pray, how to unlock the bonds, and how to guide those around you into freedom and liberty. The natural shall be shaken in the process, and it will bow to the spiritual authority of the standard I place there. Not bowing to you; bowing to My authority within you.*

*Declare, proclaim, and be aware. All the chess pieces are moving with accelerated speed, running the board victoriously with just one move. I AM peeling back the layers of unrighteousness in the earth, disclosing the very foundations of evil. My righteous standards in the earth are planted and positioned. When the sound of victory is released throughout the chambers of heaven, it will reverberate from above and below. I AM releasing that sound through the corridors of hell to announce your victory, authority, and new territory.*

*No power in hell can lift a finger against Me. Get ready for the ride of your lifetime. No more searching and asking. I AM bringing you into this crucial place of inheritance.*

## Reflecting Your Face

My identity grows stronger by overcoming, and it upgrades who I am in the Spirit. My efforts to change my behavior in order to become a new person are futile. I discover who I am in Christ and my behavior follows accordingly. When You disclose prophetically who I am, that word is designed to fast-track me into my new identity and the upgrades I am to receive. My perception of myself must align directly with Your perception. If I cannot see it, I cannot become it. When I do see it, I must agree with it and step into that identity now, for it is who I am now. When I hear it, I see it. It changes my perception of myself. I journey toward the new mindset associated with that identity and begin to think in that format, declaring that identity through my language, perceptions, and thinking.

New thinking releases new language of who I am. My natural surroundings and functions can no longer influence my thinking. I operate from Your perspective of who I am, positioning myself to bring heaven to earth with majestic thinking. As I put on the mind of Christ, I apply that mindset to confront every negative thought. I must frame every experience and challenge within the mind of Christ. Cultivate fruit within me, Father, and release Your mind and purpose through me.

I become victorious over the enemy's challenges by responding in the opposite spirit. Each challenge makes me more like You. My life is not controlled or regulated by the thoughts, actions, and opinions of people. It flourishes in Your thoughts of me. I bring my identity to the fight—every prophecy, promise, and persona word—and I begin to operate in the confidence of those words. The purpose of each circumstance is to develop me into the fulfillment of the next phase of my identity. I can be challenged only by the goodness of Your heart. Therefore, release grace upon me. See the reflection of Your face in my eyes. Old things have passed away, and all things have become new. I am a new creation. I have a new identity, a new authority, and a new placement.

Fullness is characterized by overflow. When I am overflowing with You, I am operating in fullness. Short of that overflow, I am in lack. No more settling for good when best is attainable. Overwhelm and overcome me with Your loving presence that I may be a power station of light that attracts others to You. I will arise, shine, for my light is come. I am a vessel of the miraculous release of light, love, goodness, and kindness. I no longer want to be a prisoner of ignorance. I am free to roam about the Kingdom releasing freedom and liberty from Jesus within me into those intersecting my path. Whatever is missing from my experience with You, open my eyes and heart to receive it, embrace it, walk in it, and practice it until You are satisfied.

## For Reflection

1. Do you see interruptions or "chance" meetings with others as divine appointments? What if you were to prepare your heart ahead of time to be on the lookout for them? How would that change your responses and actions?

2. Have you been fighting the battles before you, or has God? With this in mind, how can you find rest from your enemies while in the midst of your enemies?

3. After reading this chapter again, write a summary of your persona identity—how God sees you. Document it in the first person. Make it personal. Begin to release this identity into the atmosphere.

# 27

## Declarations of Identity

### I AM Statements

To go to a place where I have never been before, I must know who I am and who I am not. I will make my stand in Your glory from this place:

- I am not frightened or intimidated. I am strong and very courageous.
- I am not fearful of the future. I am excited to walk in love and faith.
- I am not controlled by my past any longer. I am a new creation full of purpose.
- I am not shackled to my old man. I am putting on the new man.
- I am no longer controlled by the flesh. I am full of the fruit of the Spirit.
- I am not discouraged or hopeless. I am full of vision and release.
- I am no longer bound by limitations. I am free to explore everything new.
- I am not silent. I am a voice and sound from heaven.
- I am not bound by sickness or disease. I am fighting from a place of wholeness.
- I am not defined or limited by my circumstances. I am a vessel of resource and blessing.

As I embrace these truths in my heart, open my eyes to see the opportunities before me. Release heaven's identity upon me and my territory. Release me. No sidetracks. No detours of my own making. If it is You, I want it.

### Remember Who You Are

I AM. *Enough said today. Remember this powerful statement of identity.* I AM. *When you are confronted with old identity issues,* remember who you are. Practice faithfulness. Practice joy in the mundane. Practice gentleness and kindness with all. Practice peace by bringing it into rest. Practice patience and self-control. Practice love by releasing the full reservoir inside you. Empty yourself to others because I AM sending you as an answer to their prayers. Do not neglect My heart for those around you, or you will miss some great opportunities necessary to connect you to your promise.

Every second is important to me, and every moment has an assignment. Ask Me who and ask Me what to release, and you will be amazed at what you hear. You are the sound to a deaf world. This sound will open the ears of the deaf to hear the sound of My voice. Be at peace; be still in steadfastness.

## For Reflection

1. Who does God say that you are?
2. What are your "I am" statements of identity from this point forward?

# 28

## What I See

### Taking On Your Features

I know I am looking more and more like You. As I am being transformed, renewed, and changed into Your likeness, the atmosphere around me is taking on the same likeness. May I just sit down in Your hands and listen to Your voice? All I desire are the mysteries and intimacies of being your closest friend. I gaze into Your beauty, fascinated with Your attention to me. Your eyes concentrate not on my imperfections but on the persona of who I am becoming. My constant gaze upon You is what transforms me into Your likeness, which in turn changes my perspective of my surroundings and circumstances.

Take me to places we have never gone before, surrounded by such beauty and transformation that it is breathtaking.

### For Reflection

1. When you look in the mirror, what do you see?
2. When you look in the spiritual mirror, what does He see?

# 29

## Follow Me, Listen, and Obey

### Lead Me

Father, I really need an abundance of wisdom right now. Turn left, turn right, go forward, stand still…. Fine-tune my ear to listen to You so I don't hear the distracting noise of the day. I want to stand still and see the salvation of the Lord, knowing I am in the right place and time. To be fully led by the Spirit is my focus.

Healing and encouragement, freedom and liberty, a future and a hope—these are all part of my persona. Clothe me in these garments and send me forth. I have been treading in deep water, developing and experiencing the refinement of preparation. But now I can sense the enormous empowerment of the great fruitfulness and release of promise. My time has come, and I desire more in this wide-open place.

### You Cannot Escape My Blessing

*Be fruitful and multiply. Release the fruit that has become part of your identity. There is no need to run ahead into the future when we can get there faster by walking through each day. Time has no meaning for Me. Timing does. I AM at work creating timely appointments that will bring you one step closer to what I have for you. Enjoy the details of each day, for I have planned each one. Grow and blossom. Dispel darkness by dispensing light and fruitfulness.*

*From this day forward, I will bless you! That is an eternal declaration. You will never be able to run fast enough ahead to overtake the blessings and favor of this day. Skip, run, stand still, bask, enjoy, embrace—it's all good. I release. You receive. I AM. You be. Exceedingly abundantly above all that you could ever imagine is yours to experience, enjoy, and elevate your confidence in Me.*

*Dream big! Then dream bigger! Take the limits off Me through your limited understanding. If you are waiting for Me to answer you in your stress and striving, you won't hear the answer. I AM calling you with sweet revelation. Put on your persona. Upgrade your thinking, perceptions, and language. Then you will hear Me loudly, clearly, and intimately.*

## For Reflection

1.  What does "be fruitful and multiply" look like in your life?
2.  Do you struggle with performance? Instead of looking at your performance, ask God to tell you how He sees you. Write it down.
3.  How do blessing and favor relate to "exceedingly abundantly"? How does "exceedingly abundantly" relate to the dreams of your heart? Look at Ephesians 3:20 and ask the Holy Spirit for new dreams and expectations.

# 30

# *Trust Me with Everything*

## All Things Serve Your Purpose

*Hebrews 10:23–24: "Let us hold fast the confession of our hope without wavering, for He who promised is faithful."*

*Hold on, and do not let go of the promise. There is a "suddenly" coming in your life. Many times My children miss blessings because impatience carries them into doubt and unbelief. Discouragement and impatience work hand in hand to divert attention from My promise and shipwreck your faith.*

*The key to holding on is being able to trust the One you are hanging onto. Do you know Me? Do you really know Me? My character is impeccable. I AM kind, merciful, trustworthy, and faithful. What I have promised, I will do. I AM not a man that I should lie, but what I say is yes and amen. You can count on Me to carry you into the fulfillment of My promise.*

*Resist the temptation to compare Me to those in your life who left you holding onto nothing but empty promises. I AM a promise-keeper; I AM a covenant-keeping God. I will not let go of your faith and trust in Me. Ever!*

*Hebrews 10:37: "For yet a little while, and He who is coming will come and will not tarry."*

*Though My promise tarries, wait patiently for it. I will come and deliver that which I promised. Take inventory of your thoughts and opinions through the lens of My grace. My grace is a game-changer and player-qualifier and is always victorious. I desire to open your eyes to the limitless possibilities and promises that are yours to explore and attain.*

*Do you understand what I AM saying? I AM releasing limitless possibilities and the fulfillment of your dreams right before your eyes. Hold fast to your faith and hope because I AM moving swiftly on your behalf. I AM releasing you into your dreams and promises by cutting you away from the old. When you experience harsh treatment from those who will not align with you or recognize who you really are, it is because they are a refining station for you. You are not meant to give your life and soul there.*

I AM *preparing your life and soul for the call of destiny over you. All things serve that purpose. All people and circumstances bow to that promise in you. Every debt and every detail that has entangled your feet, hoping to capture you in hopeless limitations, has been severed by the sword of the Spirit. Feel the release; experience the fullness of the weight of My intentions for you. Receive ALL I have for you. Pick up your tent and your stakes and get ready to drive them more deeply into My promises for the present-future. Do not be influenced by the opinions of others or the decisions they make. They all serve My purposes, and you will see this more clearly when you look through the lens of My Spirit.*

## My Response to You

I so appreciate Your patience and kindness with me. I find renewed strength when I read this love song over me. It brings boldness in my faith and renewed confidence in Your word over me. Many times the natural problems of the psalmist David's environment drove him into the shelter of the secret place. His psalms describe the emotional roller coaster. But once in Your secret place, he was changed and transformed by Your presence. He always left in a better place than when he arrived.

Like David, I came to You this morning with heaviness and despondence, but I am entering my day with renewed confidence and strength from the secret place with You. You are my Deliverer today, my refuge and strength, my high tower of refuge, the Rock on which I stand, the hope that encompasses me, my favor and glory, the lifter of my head.

"Touch not My anointed," says the Lord. I am a baby cub, standing upright but small in stature, growling at the predator standing before me, not realizing that the mother bear, extreme in height, power, and authority, towers behind me. The enemy is paralyzed when he sees You standing behind me, knowing that You live within me. Insulate me and protect me with Your care over me. I love You. I encourage myself in You.

## For Reflection

1. Make a list of people and situations that have seemed negative to you. Ask God to show you how they have served His purpose for you. Write those responses down.

2. Have you asked God what purpose you serve in the lives of those around you? Because God has placed you there, what is God asking you to be for those in your life?

# 31

## Divine Intersections

### Just Be, And Let Me

I have awakened to the summons of Your heart. As I release all
that You have placed within me, take every part of my soul and
baptize it in Your Holy Spirit, drenching me under the waterfall of
total fullness. I am all Yours and not my own. I love You and cannot
help but keep saying this. My only desire from this day forward is to
be the pliable clay that You can form for every intersecting moment.

Make me a Philip who was translated to carry Your presence
where it was needed. You can trust me to bring Your presence into
any part of the earth. Such glorious presence is washing over me this
morning. Let the gushing rain wash over me. Then spark the flame
of promise into an uncontrollable fire. Enlarge my capacity for more
love. I cannot love You enough. Bring Your cloud of glory over my
steps today.

### High Expectations

I AM *weeping in joy with you as My heart has been touched by the
brokenness in you. You have crossed into a place of no return. My
glory has an appointment with you. Just step into it. My glory has
been scheduled to change and transform everything of purpose. I AM
bringing strategic change and shifts this day, and I have also scheduled
this Philip appointment to speak into the lives I bring to you today.
Just be. And let Me.*

*When you come to the place in your spirit where you are willing
to invest My resources in the strategic targets where My glory dwells,
a release will take place automatically in the Spirit. Withholding
the fulfillment of your highest expectations has not been because I
AM waiting on a performance improvement to pour out My blessing.
Not this day. I have been withholding until I gather the most targets
possible within your sight.*

*As I release this increase, know that you have asked for an amount
that equates only to today's need. I want you to ask for more than this.*

*I want you to ask for the never-ending rain of abundance. Ask big; then ask bigger. From this day forward, I will bless you. Expect it. Take it to the bank.*

*Listen to this sound—not the one in your slightly distant past that screams poverty and caution, but the sound of your future that shouts abundance. Expect My resources in ways you would not have thought possible. Keep sowing and investing in My Kingdom, and I will keep returning. Keep pressing, and I will keep pouring. Keep asking, and I will always answer.*

## For Reflection

1. Are you listening to sounds of accusation from the past, or have you positioned yourself to hear your identity from God's perspective?
2. What areas of your life do you have yet to surrender in order to be a Philip vessel (Acts 8:26–40)? Ask God to take those unsurrendered areas and transform them into willingness to be everything God wants you to be.

# 32

## Singing a New Song

### Putting Words to Action

I speak and declare life over the territories my feet walk on today. No more curse of death or unguarded openings for the enemy to tear the social fabric of the family through tragedy and sorrow. I declare life, life, life—resurrection life. You have enlarged my spiritual territory to include places where death has been present and destruction prevalent. My tent has been enlarged, my ropes lengthened, and my stakes reestablished and driven deeper. I am clearing the ground for expansion and fulfillment. Territory is a bounty that is mine. New beginnings have begun and new territory is available to conquer.

Therefore I will sing in my barren state and sing as never before. My song permeates the atmosphere and penetrates the territory of unfulfilled promise, declaring the word of the Lord over my world. I am preparing the soil of my heart to receive and to give away. My dreams of expansion, blessing, favor, and freedom from captivity awaken in me a generous place of high expectation. You enlarge my place to receive more of You by dislodging and removing all the residual unbelief and callousness of heart.

As I pound my stakes of expansion into the ground, I am striking those stakes deep into the heart of my past. Embarrassment, lack, insecurity, humiliation—all are being severed by the stakes driven into the hearts of these areas.

Deep inside these areas are transformational seeds of greatness. This severing from my past has opened those seeds of greatness to breathe and grow into my true identity. No more embarrassment, only proclamation of Your greatness. No more lack, only the great fruit of Your bounty lavished on me and stored for me as gifts from Your throne. No more insecurity, only great confidence in You to guide, direct, and minister through me, so I will never again be disabled by doubt. No more humiliation, only great exaltation before people and before God, because Christ inside me is righteous and deserving. This is what it means to think big. You are a big God with a big heart.

## For Reflection

1. Ask God what your territory and bounty are for the future. Write it down. Each day, review and release it into the atmosphere by declaring your authority in this realm. This is your new song to sing.

2. What areas in your life have robbed you of your new song? They have now become your audience. Stare them down and sing the words of your future.

# 33

## Building the New Man

### Fruitfulness

Fruitfulness is a tell-all. It tells me where I am in my development. You graciously release life's exercises and pop quizzes to assign the fruit of the Spirit to each problem. In the Kingdom, two things should be clearly visible after I face the giant before me: the carcass of the enemy and the fruit of the Spirit that defeated him. While I have not experienced the fullness of Your release, I am quickly moving into position to receive it, strengthened in my upgrades and in the fruit of the Spirit.

We are building the new man, Father, one brick at a time, creating a fortress of worship.

### Every Second Has a Purpose

*Walk humbly before Me and deeper into the pools of My fullness. You can pour out only what you have inside. You will release this glory and favor wherever you go; and people, cities, and nations will be changed. This is your inheritance, beloved, and it is an inheritance that can be given away without depleting it one iota.*

*You are a vessel of multiplication, not addition. Accelerated empowerment is accelerated positioning to target everything and everyone with lightning strikes of My presence. Have purpose in every breath. Every second has a purpose now. That is what it means to pray without ceasing.*

### For Reflection

1. Have you asked God what His inheritance is for you? What has been His response?
2. Take inventory of your spiritual development every day. What does it mean to "move into position to receive increased fruitfulness"?

# 34

# *You Are My Ready Weapon of Choice*

## You Are My Lord

My heart is Yours. I cannot govern my life or its direction through my own understanding. You have placed me in places too wonderful for me to understand—wide-open places of exploration and discovery.

In this place, You are the Captain every day. Every day, every breath, You are my Lord. Without You, my life lacks meaning.

## Preparation Is About to Meet Opportunity

*I have the most amazing places for you. Jump out into the unknown and I will do the life-changing. Launch out, jump off, step into new places of exploration. I AM taking you into a place of trust in this hour. We will have fun together as you begin to understand how I AM orchestrating this new place. In the little things, the big things, and all in between. Just believe!*

*I AM here and will never abandon or ignore you. I AM here. I AM the Faithful One. Yeshua, Jesus, your Beloved. Fear not! For you were born and equipped for such a time as this. Stake your ground! Don't give up! Don't quit! You have been equipped for such a time as this. Get your eyes off the past and look forward. Don't slack, because there is a dance with your name on it.*

*By the words of your declaration, you will walk through an open door of advancement. Preparation is about to meet opportunity. Divine favor is yours. I AM carrying you through doors on the wings of My Spirit, undetected by the enemy. I AM releasing strategies yet unformed and unknown. Wonders, signs, and miracles are the fruit because I AM the Source of it all.*

*Watch how I blend things to create My greatest surprises for you. This is not a time to quit; it is a time to equip. Quitting is not in your DNA. I have designed you to rule and reign with Me. It is time to be fruitful and multiply. It is time to be fruitful and be multiplied. Everything you experience serves My eternal purpose for you.*

*Release the preemptive strikes of intercession I have put deep within you. The enemy is frightened of who you are. He will use everything possible to shut you down because you carry the answer for this hour. Arise and be what I created you to be. Set the captives free. I have sounded the alarm in heaven announcing the release of My glory in the earth. All My strategically planted vessels will now arise, shine, for their life purpose has come. Plant intercession and declare the answer through the fruit that you bear. This is your year of double maturity. My mercy is new every morning, and I cover you in the richness of that mercy. My mercy and love protect you from your greatest fears.*

## For Reflection

1. What would "launch out, jump off, step into new places of exploration" mean for you in your life?
2. Can you look back at the past seasons of your life and identify the areas of preparation you have experienced? How was God preparing you?

# 35

## *Grow into Your Destiny*

### Isaiah 54 Coronation

*"Enlarge the place of your tent, and let them stretch out the curtains of your dwellings; do not spare; lengthen your cords, and strengthen your stakes. For you shall expand to the right and to the left, and your descendants will inherit the nations, and make the desolate cities inhabited.*

*"Do not fear, for you will not be ashamed; neither be disgraced, for you will not be put to shame; for you will forget the shame of your youth, and will not remember the reproach of your widowhood anymore. For your Maker is your husband, the LORD of Hosts is His name; and your Redeemer is the Holy One of Israel; He is called the God of the whole earth. For the LORD has called you like a woman forsaken and grieved in spirit, like a youthful wife when you were refused," says your God.*

*"For a mere moment I have forsaken you, but with great mercies I will gather you. With a little wrath I hid My face from you for a moment; but with everlasting kindness I will have mercy on you," says the LORD, your Redeemer.*

*"For this is like the waters of Noah to Me; for as I have sworn that the waters of Noah would no longer cover the earth, so have I sworn that I would not be angry with you, nor rebuke you. For the mountains shall depart and the hills be removed, but My kindness shall not depart from you, nor shall My covenant of peace be removed," says the LORD, who has mercy on you....*

*"In righteousness you shall be established; you shall be far from oppression, for you shall not fear; and from terror, for it shall not come near you. Indeed they shall surely assemble, but not because of Me. Whoever assembles against you shall fall for your sake....*

*"No weapon formed against you shall prosper, and every tongue which rises against you in judgment you shall condemn. This is the*

*heritage of the servants of the LORD, and their righteousness is from Me," says the LORD.*

*Isaiah 54:2–10, 14–15, 17*

## Expansion

Father, how precious these words are as I step across new thresholds. My identity is wrapped up in these ancient words of knowledge. I will sing as I welcome all You are sending to me. I will not spare; and whatever You ask, I will do. Teach me; and open wisdom, understanding, and a teachable spirit within me. Expansion makes demands on inheritance.

I have been called up, but not from the mountaintop. I have been called up and summoned from the low areas and opinions of myself. It may have seemed for a short time as if I was forsaken, but never have You been closer. I am stepping into a newer dimension of everlasting kindness. Your kindness is of the same proportion as You showed Noah, for this everlasting kindness is filled with peace and mercy. I have crossed over into understanding the rightful place and heritage I have in You.

## For Reflection

1. What areas of your life are being expanded? Are you aware of the promises in Isaiah 54 that come with expansion? Which promises are you hanging onto in this passage?
2. Have you considered that expansion can unlock your inheritance? How does this fit in your life?
3. Rewrite those sections of Isaiah 54 in the first person, and read this declaration over your life. For example: "I will enlarge the place of my tent. I will stretch out the curtains of my dwelling." (Please continue.)

# 36

# The Release of Covenant Promise

## Covenant Glory

Bring fast finishes to yesterday and quick starting points of new beginnings. When I see a cloud passing through the blue sky, I cannot see its speed, only the distance it has traveled. Accelerate me in the same way, where I focus not on the speed of the journey but on the distance covered through the process of growth. As I embrace the process, may I look up and be suddenly and pleasantly surprised by the clouds of Your covenant surrounding me.

As Your covenant covers me, multiply all the seed that has been planted. Multiply that seed exponentially to catapult me into my life mission. You are clearing out the atmosphere in the physical realm. Do the same in every area of my life—over my finances, declare Your covenant of increase and fruitfulness. Cancel my debts through the jubilee of Your grace. Command health over my mind and body to align with Your Kingdom purpose. Transport me into my future.

A shift has begun, out of the soul and into the spirit, out of the natural realm and into the supernatural. All the promises and declarations, all the revelation and game-planning, all the encouraging prophetic words given and received—seal them all with a visible downpour of Your covenant of multiplication.

## Standing in the Glory Together

*Stand still and see the salvation* I AM *performing. Listen to the sounds of My release. I* AM *surrounding you in covenant. Think bigger. Don't lock Me into a scrawny personal box. I release covenant blessing, and no matter which direction you go, you will be protected by it. Every thought and action shall exude fruitfulness. They will come into alignment with My covenant. Every desire and passion I have put into your heart is a covenant expression.*

*All heaven and earth adore Me, for* I AM *great and greatly to be praised! You are standing in the glory of My presence, in the middle* of My cloud. Rain is seen around you but not on you. Freedom, faith, grace, and favor are all here. We are standing in the glory together. We will go to a place you have never been before.

I AM high and lifted up. My house is filled with smoke, the shekinah glory. I AM filling your temple with My shekinah glory that changes and transforms you into My purpose.

## For Reflection

1. Repeat out loud the conversation to the Lord above. Read it as your own. Then ask God to show you how to align with the benefits of His covenant blessing over you.
2. Pen His response back to you. If you don't hear anything, read it again and ask God to speak to your heart. Write down your impressions.

# 37

## Perfect Peace and Rest in Transformation

### Transformed in My Courts

Lord, help me understand the times, that I may be wise in my approach. All that You have stored up for me is coming forth. I am blessed beyond comprehension. Door after door is opening, and my intimacy with You shows me the right door to walk through. According to the word that You covenanted with me, You are blessing me. From this day forward, You are blessing me. In all things, I give thanks.

Lord, I am designed to work from a place of rest. When I begin to look at the future with excitement, help me not to overthink things, overanalyze details, and overstep my place in Your perfect will. Because You have established me in Your courts of worship, I am at perfect peace and rest. Viewing things from the perspective of heaven is my default position. Your sweet presence shields me from the heat of the day, the darts of my enemies, and the self-inflicted doubt of the soul. Show me what You want to work on today. What part of me do You wish to address?

Transform my negative thoughts and actions by the fruit of Your Spirit that will reframe my thinking and responses. Your majesty and fullness leave no empty place. Multiply the fruit and promise deposited for such a time as this. I am abiding in You, abounding in fruitfulness, and abolishing every negative thought and action by applying my promises and dreams to them. I am assimilating a life of honor, full of the anointing of the Holy Spirit. This is my lot, my inheritance. Give me the fullness of my inheritance.

I give You everything. I am going to a place I have never been before. I am standing in Your glory. This is my default position.

## For Reflection

1. Evaluate your perspective of God and who He is in your life. How does your perspective differ when you enter the courts of worship with Him?

2. What areas of your old nature need to be transformed? Inventory the areas you are struggling with. Read Galatians 5:16–26 and write down the fruit of the Spirit next to each area of struggle you are experiencing. Ask God to create opportunities to develop each one of these fruits.

# 38

# The Song of Worship

## Receiving Communion

As I take Communion today, I receive. But it seems backwards. Shouldn't You be receiving from me? In essence, I give all of me for all of You—at least, all that I know to give—but I want to give You more and I don't know what that looks like. My willingness to give has opened my spirit to receive. Giving You everything I know to give, I realize that You gave Your everything for me. In the Garden, You sweat great drops of blood, not only because of the pain of the cross, but also because of Your upcoming separation from the Father.

This causes me to stop and thank You for enduring that awful pain of abandonment so I never have to. That understanding helps me receive everything I need from You. You have already gone through the process of separation, isolation, and preparation so I can live in the 24-7 security of Your presence.

As I take Communion today, every wall of separation has been broken in two and crumbled into ruins. I am fully and completely united with You. As I eat and drink in remembrance of You, I receive this greatest love from You. I receive Your wholeness that releases complete healing for sickness and disease. Your stripes and horrible beating have paid that debt in full. I receive wisdom and revelation for my mind in need of renewal. I receive deliverance for financial freedom, announcing the year of jubilee release over me. I receive full restoration of all relationships.

As You look down upon me with this freedom, I look into Your eyes and cry. This day, I am drenched in Your goodness and kindness. I could never earn Your goodness with my performance but I receive Your scepter extended to me because of my identity as Your son. I run toward You, Father, and throw my arms around Your neck. My tears saturate Your chest. I am Yours. Completely.

## The Power of the Sound of Unity

*The sound coming from your worship is causing a rumbling and quaking in the Spirit realm that is deafening to the enemy. These united sounds of worship are accentuated and amplified to echo My majesty throughout eternity. That sound chases the enemy as a predator chases its prey. Echoes of resilient praise pass through the eternal corridors of the Spirit with the power of an exploding fire incinerating everything in its path.*

*My daughters and sons unite in a melodious song that causes Me to arise and dance. My glory has reached its tipping point, and your song, like a fiery lava descending the hill of the Lord, has produced a thick, rich love full of the fruit of the Spirit that will escort My glory through you upon the earth. Your song has moved Me.*

## For Reflection

1. Take a quiet moment and, with a heart of thankfulness, offer up to God your best gift: you. Name the areas of your life that you will present to Him as an offering of honor.
2. What is the divine exchange between you and God? What are you giving and receiving from Him? What is He giving and receiving from you? This has become a song to the Lord.

# 39

## Expanded through Upgraded Understanding

### Renewed Thinking Creates Clearer Vision

Father, I will meditate on the Word You have given me. I will eat Your Word and absorb its richness. The eyes of my soul will search for the fulfillment of Your Word in my upgraded thinking. I speak to the seat of my emotions: *Come under the authority of the Word my Father has spoken, and be calm. Be quiet.*

I will "see the goodness of the LORD in the land of the living" (Psalm 27:13). When I lie down, I will not be afraid but enjoy sweet rest (Proverbs 3:24).

My crooked places are becoming straight. Make me into a testimony of Your goodness, kindness, mercy, and deliverance. I cast all my anxieties, cares, frets, and "what-ifs" onto You in surrender. I no longer want ownership of those areas of my life. I give them to You. You hold my future full of hope and promise. You. Only You. My crooked thinking is aligned with my vertical relationship with You as I upgrade my mind, will, and emotions in my new man identity.

You have put Your finger lovingly upon the areas of my life You have appointed for change. No longer fighting the rescue, no longer resisting You as my lifeguard, I have become still in the waters of life. When I begin to sink, I cry out, my hand outstretched, knowing that You are there to draw me up out of the treacherous waters. You lift me out, reminding me that I do not belong beneath the waters but on them.

No more self-reliance. No more fighting or striving to remain afloat despite the swallowing forces around me. Surrender. Floating. Waiting. Worshiping. This is my new season. I will not drown in the waters of yesterday's impossibilities and identity. You have prepared me for this moment.

The multiplication of fruitfulness is stretching out the curtains of my dwellings. More than one dwelling. Dwellings. Plural. I will not be spare but allow my spheres of influence to stretch me into a larger source of encouragement, mentoring, and service. I stretch out the cords that have tied me to the safe, comfortable living I have become accustomed to this past season. I enlarge my influence and tighten every area of slack. I strengthen my stakes by driving them deeper into the grounded word of Your promise. Stability through a deeper foundation of strength.

In order to carry the weight of Your glory, favor, and blessing, I must enlarge my foundation to carry Your presence. There must be a large enough place for You to rest upon. I will not fear, because You promised that I will not be disgraced, neither will I be put to shame. I forget the past shame as I embrace the fruitfulness of my new season of life.

You are my husband, protector, provider, security. You have called me. I am redeemed, therefore, purchased back for this specific time in my life. Even though there have been times when I felt forsaken and abandoned to widowhood, it is by Your great mercy that I am gathered back to You. You never remove Your kindness because we have covenanted together. Never again will I experience separation from Your kindness. It is mine—the fullness of it. I want all of You.

## For Reflection

1. Do you have areas of your life that are not yet fully submitted to God? What are they?
2. What part do you play in your vertical relationship with God to upgrade your mind, will and emotions? What part does God play?

# 40

## I Will Point You to Others

### Release Anointing

Father, I am blown away at the favor upon favor upon favor that You are releasing. I cannot even begin to list all the things You are doing in my life. You have stretched me into my Isaiah 54 season as never before. You have summoned me out of prison and brought me forth to stand before You.

*You have conquered the schemes of the devil at this level. I will be with you in this new place, throughout this time of extreme stretching. When you begin to feel your self-imposed walls close in on you, remember that I am with You. Chill out and watch Me work. I work best when you and I face your impossibilities together, and you look to Me quickly for help. I cannot help but answer you and show My glory and favor. I have promised to bless you from this day forward. Just go and release it. Expect angelic presence. I will do something different in the days ahead from what you expect.*

Holy Spirit, You bring back remembrance of the Word inside me. Release the power of the living God. Establish every step I take with every word that conceives a promise, and piece them together like a mosaic reflecting Your glory. Let it be here on earth as it is in heaven—an open corridor of Your presence that reflects the true light and nothing else.

The sharp division created by My Word will cut through the hard layers of old thinking. I AM awakening your state and your nation with a new revelation of My presence. My presence will not run like a stream. Instead it will be a rushing torrent taking out every obstruction to new man thinking. I AM kicking old man thinking to the curb. It is time to move out because I AM coming in. Be at rest and release My anointing that I have poured into you. It will be like the wedding feast at Cana where I turned water to wine. I AM filling every water vessel full of new wine, new silver and new gold. This will be a "Wow!" time.

You are too good to me, Lord. I cannot help but cry because Your goodness is too good, Your kindness is too kind. Do not expand my territory if You don't expand my passion for You. It has to burn within me from the depths of my heart. I am overwhelmed and undone as I anticipate the fulfillment of Your personal word over me. Drip down on all the territory You show me. As I walk through my day, qualify all that territory as my inheritance. Face to face, cheek to cheek, love complete in Jesus' name.

## Commissioned to Release

*My ears are always attentive to the needy. My compassion and love for all mankind run deeper than human understanding.* I AM *commissioning you to release the same compassion by seeing others the way I see them. As I did with you, I do not see what is wrong with them, only what is missing. I call you to see others the same way and call them to their identity and purpose. Instead of looking at the many faults and dysfunctional behaviors of the broken, ask Me to show you what I see when I look at them.*

*Be the beam of light they reach toward that pulls them up. Be an illustration of the extended mercies of My heart. In the process, become a life-giver and a life-changer.*

## For Reflection

1. Are you stuck in unfulfilled expectations? Maybe they are the wrong ones. Ask God to reveal a new understanding of what He wants to release to you. As you listen to Him quietly, pen those expectations as your declarations of expectation.

2. In what ways can you become a vessel of life to those around you? What parts of your old nature have to lose their influence over you in order to become this abundant vessel of life? Ask God to reveal these truths through Isaiah 58:6–11.

# *In Conclusion*

It is my prayer that this book of intimate conversations with God has sparked the flames of intimacy He desires to have with you. Getting started is always the hardest thing to do. How can you develop your own conversations with Him? Here are just a few things I have learned in my journal time with Him.

1. Do not become discouraged with what your words look like. God is not looking for conversations with great writers. He is interested in connecting with you in your current situation.
2. Establish a routine early in the morning or late at night where you can avoid distractions. Time spent is not as important as quality time invested. I began with 20 minutes early in the morning, and it has increased substantially because it was the quality of intimacy I was experiencing.
3. Find a quiet place where you can be free to reflect. My wife and I have designated a specific area in our house called the secret place where we can pray and study.
4. Be honest. God knows your heart, and more importantly, He wants you to know it. Being transparent in your words to Him in how you feel and where you are going is critical in understanding who He wants to be for you.
5. How do you hear God? This may be different for everyone. Before you begin your conversation with Him, ask the Holy Spirit to speak to you. Just begin to write from your heart. The Holy Spirit will disclose everything the Father has to say.
6. The length of the conversation is not as important as the intimacy and honesty of it. Apply the truths and promises of His Word directly to your circumstances. God has your promises and answers hidden deep in the secret place of relationship with you.
7. Why write your conversations? I learned through my training as a school administrator that writing is the highest cognitive skill there is because it causes you to slow down, gather your thoughts, and pen your words. The process lends itself to deeper thought and contemplation. It is not your mastery in

writing that is important. It is the depth of relationship as you commune with God.

8. Keeping a journal allowed me to revisit my conversations with Him, especially when I was struggling. It reset my focus.

God desires to have a close relationship with His children. To dance on the waters with Him is to simply get out of the boat and move toward Him. He will not let you fail, and He will not let you go under. Like He did with Peter, He immediately reached His hand down to pick Him back up as he began to sink. Jesus was not condemning Peter with the words, "O ye of little faith." Jesus was encouraging Peter to grow in his faith with the future assurance that Jesus would always be there on the waters with him through every new encounter. Getting out of the boat and onto the waters with Him positions us to find and fulfill our destiny and purpose. I am finding mine through my intimate conversations with Him. How about you?